What
Do You
Really
Want?

What Do You Really Want?

St. Ignatius Loyola
and the Art
of Discernment

JIM MANNEY

ISBN: 978-1-61278-796-1 (Inventory No. T1602)
eISBN: 978-1-61278-365-9
LCCN: 2015932828

Cover design: Amanda Falk
Cover art: St. Ignatius of Loyola (oil on canvas), Italian School, (17th century) / © Rochdale Art Gallery, Lancashire, UK / Bridgeman Images
Interior design: Dianne Nelson

PRINTED IN THE UNITED STATES OF AMERICA

Endorsements for
What Do You Really Want?

Jim Manney has a profound grasp of Ignatian spirituality and
an uncanny ability to make it available to readers of our age.
This book will help you to make decisions that bring more
profound satisfaction and put you on God's side in the great
work of bringing about God's kingdom. Like Ignatian spirituality itself this book can't just be read; it has to be lived.
— **William A. Barry, S.J., author of** *The Practice of*
Spiritual Direction **and** *Letting God Come Close*

Jim Manney's *What Do You Really Want?* asks what is probably the most important question in the spiritual life, the
question that pushes us to go deeper than what the noise of
the world tells us we must do if we are to be happy, wealthy,
or admired. Spend some time with this book, written by
a canny guide to the spiritual life who is happy to remind
us that he is on the shoulders of giants. If you are new to
prayer, this book will help you understand more about how
it makes us practiced in the art of making life choices. If you
are experienced, you'll appreciate the clarity that Manney
brings to deepening your discernment, using St. Ignatius as a
guide.
— **Tim Muldoon, author of** *The Ignatian Workout* **and**
The Ignatian Workout for Lent

What Do You Really Want? translates the nuances of Ignatian
spirituality into an understandable and practical guide for
anyone seeking to live a spiritual life. Jim Manney's expla-
nations of Ignatian discernment and decision making offer
new insights and cultural translations to 500-year old wisdom of the Spiritual Exercises.
— **Lisa Kelly, Ignatian Associate, dotMagis blogger**

This straightforward yet highly nuanced and comprehensive text will reward the reader rich guidance for prayer and discernment, no matter their level of spiritual practice. God comes alive in these pages for a reader seeking to initiate or deepen their love for their creator and sanctifier. Take up and read, and may Jesus bless your journey.

— **Ben Hawley, S.J., director of Catholic Campus Ministry, University of Michigan**

Jim Manney has written a concise, balanced, and wise set of reflections on Ignatian discernment and decision making. This is a study that will prove most helpful either as an introduction to the tradition or as a stimulating review to those more familiar with the art of discernment. Besides a sure understanding of the Ignatian practice of discernment, Manney constantly casts a keen pastoral eye on its significance in trying to live a full Christian life today.

— **Howard Gray, S.J., special assistant to the president, Georgetown University**

Jim Manney distills the essential lessons of Ignatian discernment in a way that is both faithful to the tradition and applicable to the present day. He writes clearly, concisely, and passionately about a subject he loves. This book will be a great help to people who are striving to root their decision making in their faith.

— **Kevin O'Brien, S.J., vice president for Mission and Ministry at Georgetown University and author of** *The Ignatian Adventure: Experiencing the Spiritual Exercises of Saint Ignatius in Daily Life*

Contents

1

Discernment As a Way of Life

What should I be doing? Maybe this is not such a pressing question for you. You might think you know perfectly well what to do, mainly what *others* want you to do—bosses, spouses, children, parents, the government. The problem is getting it all done, and when you have some free time, you do what you want to do without a lot of fuss and deep thought. But most of us ask this question periodically. Occasionally it becomes a very important question; we face big decisions about how we should spend our time and money, about new jobs and career changes, about intractable family problems, about dilemmas involving work colleagues and friends. The question "What should I be doing?" rumbles in the background as we go about our everyday tasks: how to tackle the to-do list at home and at work, how much to spend on clothes and entertainment and food, when to drop in on that sick neighbor or make that phone call you've been putting off, how to love the people we love, how to love the people who drive us nuts.

Christians need to take these questions seriously. From one point of view, finding good answers to them *is* the Christian life, at least the Christian life as we live it on the ground every day. Striving to live as a Christian means finding the best ways to respond in love in our concrete circumstances. Life presents us with a never-ending succession of opportunities to bring the love of God to others, to act virtuously, to do the work of Christ. "Everywhere there is good to be done," said St. Peter Faber. "Everywhere there is something to be planted and harvested." We are constantly making choices about these things. As we make them we gradually become the kind of person God meant us to be.

As Christians we believe that God will help us make these choices. Jesus promised it: "The Advocate, the Holy Spirit, whom the Father will send in my name, will teach you everything, and remind you of all that I have said to you" (Jn 14:26). Christians have invoked God's help in making decisions from the very beginning. The first thing the apostles did after Jesus's Ascension was to choose someone to replace Judas as a member of the Twelve. They nominated two men and prayed, "Lord, you know everyone's heart. Show us which one of these two you have chosen to take the place in this ministry" (Acts 1:25). Ever since, Christians have prayed for God's guidance. The Holy Spirit is active in our lives. If we call on him, and learn how to listen, we will be guided in our choices. We will be able to know what God wants.

"Examine everything carefully," Paul writes to the Thessalonians (see 1 Thes 5:21). "Test the spirits to see whether they are from God," says the apostle John (1 Jn 4:1). Over the centuries, the Church has developed a deep understanding of how to do this. This is discernment, a skill and an art, an essentially spiritual process rooted in prayer, but also a methodology, something we can learn about, and get better at over time.

WHAT IS DISCERNMENT?

The root of the word "discernment" is the Latin word *discerno,* meaning to sever or separate. It's essentially the ability to separate what's important from what's irrelevant or misleading. One of the complaints sometimes heard about it is that the word "discernment" doesn't have much real content, that it amounts to little more than common sense enlightened by faith. St. Ignatius

Loyola, whose ideas about discernment we will follow closely in this book, thought otherwise. He used the word to mean both keenness of insight and skill in discriminating. It's first *seeing*, then *interpreting* what is perceived. He thought that the ability to discern the spirits was one of the most important skills that a Christian can have.

Ignatian discernment is often thought to be synonymous with Ignatian decision making. Discernment is an important part of making good decisions—a necessary part in the Ignatian view—but discernment is something much broader. "Testing the spirits," as scripture has it, is something that should go on all the time. God is always present in our world; the Holy Spirit is constantly active in our inner life. Other spirits are active too — "the enemy of our human nature," as Ignatius put it. Discernment means tuning into this spiritual maelstrom and finding the way God is leading us. Discernment can help us with big decisions, but discernment is also active when we're standing in a supermarket checkout line, sitting in a business meeting, and listening to a friend's tale of woe.

In the Ignatian view, discernment is a state of reflective awareness of the spiritual significance of things. It's a kind of detached engagement with the world, a way of being actively involved in life from a position of thoughtful sensitivity to spiritual realities. The Ignatian ideal is to be a "contemplative in action," someone constantly attuned to the inner life as they continually seek to bring the love of God to the people and circumstances they encounter every day. When we become proficient at discernment, it becomes a way of life.

WHAT IGNATIUS DISCOVERED

Our mentor for discernment is Ignatius Loyola, founder of the Jesuits, author of the *Spiritual Exercises,* and a major figure in both secular and religious history. The Jesuits became a world-wide missionary order, a major force in the sixteenth-century renewal of Catholicism, and the creators of an educational system that transformed Europe and beyond. Ignatian spirituality has had an enormous impact, spreading far beyond the Jesuits. It has shaped the outward-oriented, active outlook that is characteristic of much modern spirituality. Many think that Ignatius's *Spiritual Exercises* is the single most influential book on prayer and the spiritual life ever written.

Ignatian spirituality is rooted in an experience of conversion that Ignatius had at the age of thirty. Born to minor nobility in the Basque region of northern Spain, the young Ignatius led a disorderly life as a courtier at the court of Navarre and later as a knight in the duke's army. In 1521 he was seriously wounded in battle and spent a year convalescing at home. There he had an experience of profound conversion to Christ. He abandoned his military career, renounced the privileges of his social class, and embarked on the path that led him to become one the Church's greatest innovators and spiritual writers.

Ignatius's key insight was that God speaks to us through the shifting sea of feelings, insights, leadings, and intuitions of our affective lives. Our desires are of particular importance. We are led astray by "disordered attachments"—desires that mislead us and crowd out our deepest, truest desires. The deepest desires are to know and serve God. The choices we make are about how to best fulfill these desires in the concrete circumstances of our lives. Ignatius believed that our deepest desires were placed in our hearts by God. So, when we discover what we really want, we discover what God wants too.

Ignatius's ideas about discernment (and much more) are found in the *Spiritual Exercises*. In the *Spiritual Exercises* we meet Christ inviting each of us to find our place in his work of saving and healing the world. Ignatius would have us ask three questions: "What have I done for Christ? What am I doing for

Christ? What ought I do for Christ?" Discernment has a very important role in our answers to these questions. Finding the work we're meant to do requires discernment—the attentiveness to the inner life where we can find God's leading.

Ignatius's ideas about discernment are distilled into twenty-two "rules for the discernment of spirits" that he appended to the end of the *Spiritual Exercises*. We will go through these rules in some detail in this book, but we will also look at some of the other ideas in the *Spiritual Exercises* that put discernment in the right context and provide the foundation for it.

First—a few words about the *Spiritual Exercises*. The *Spiritual Exercises* is not a book that you would pick up for inspiring spiritual reading. The book the *Spiritual Exercises* is the outline for an intensive retreat-prayer experience, also known as the Spiritual Exercises. Ignatius wrote the book for spiritual directors who lead people through this retreat. In Ignatius's day, the usual form of the Spiritual Exercises was an intensive thirty-day retreat. Today the Exercises are usually given over the course of many months in a format that allows people to continue with their normal activities.

Ignatius designed the Exercises to bring about a deep conversion to Christ and his work. "Design" isn't quite the right word for what Ignatius did. The Spiritual Exercises (and the rules for discernment) are the fruit of years of patient observation and trial and error as Ignatius worked to help people grow closer to God. He didn't design a program as much as he discovered spiritual truths and principles of human psychology that have always been true. His great accomplishment was to assemble these truths into a coherent package, which became the basis for a powerful program of conversion.

The empirical origins of Ignatian spirituality is one reason for its practicality. It's not burdened with theory, and it doesn't call on people to scale rarified spiritual heights. It is centered on the person of Jesus. Its aim is to help us join Christ's work in the world and thereby come to know and love him more deeply. One of the mottos of Ignatian spirituality is "finding God in all things." This implies that the good is plural. There are many ways to God.

Ignatian discernment is practical too. Some complain that the discernment they are familiar with is vague and subjective. Ignatian discernment is neither. It is a skill and a methodology. The skill part is about acquiring habits of prayerful attentiveness and learning how to interpret spiritual senses and inner movements of the heart. The methodology is applying these skills (and other tools) to the choices and decisions we face in real life. Discernment is hard to define, but here's a stab at it: Discernment is the wisdom that enables us to distinguish between feelings, ideas, and motives that are from the Holy Spirit and those that aren't. It shows us the choices that lead to God and those that don't.

WHY OUR CHOICES MATTER

Let's begin with a fundamental question—the question that philosophy and theology begin with. Why are we here? Ignatius gave his answer in a short passage at the beginning of the *Spiritual Exercises* called The First Principle and Foundation. The first sentence answers the question "Why are we here?" *"Man is created to praise, reverence, and serve God our Lord, and by this means to save his soul."* This tells us what we're on earth to do, but it tells us other things too. It tells us that we are *created* to do this. That is, the deepest, truest truth about us is that God created us to praise, reverence, and serve him. This is what we really want. This is what God really wants too. The seeds of the answer to the eternal question "What is God's will?" lie in that sentence. We will know what God wants when we know what we really want.

What it means to love God varies from time to time and place to place and person to person. We live in a world of vast complexity. The First Principle and Foundation continues:

> The other things on the face of the earth are created for man to help him in attaining the end for which he is created. Hence, man is to make use of them in as far as they help him in the attainment of his end, and he must rid himself of them in as far as they prove a hindrance to him.

This is how we are to love and serve God. The way to God is through the "things on the face of the earth." God is not "up there." He is *here*—in the work we do, our friends and family, our responsibilities, our ambitions and hopes and disappointments, the opportunities and misfortunes that come our way, the way we interact with the institutions of society. Nothing is so small, so fleeting, so distasteful, or so awful that it's excluded from God's love. All of it is meaningful. All of it has the potential to take us to God.

It follows that the choices we make about these things are just about the most important things we do. Here is the great challenge of life: to choose the good (*"make use of them in as far as they help him in the attainment of his end"*) and avoid the bad (*"rid himself of them in as far as they prove a hindrance to him"*). This is why our choices matter, and this is where discernment comes in. It points the way toward the choices that will bring us closer to the end for which we were created.

CHOOSING THE GOOD

Ignatius assumes—and we assume here too—that people interested in discernment have committed themselves to pursuing the good. He says that those who want to do the Exercises should "enter upon them with magnanimity and generosity" toward God. Discernment is not for people who are deceiving others, entangled in crime, engaged in malicious behavior, or are otherwise walking on the dark side. It's irrelevant for people who aren't sure whether they want the good at all. This doesn't mean that we have to attain a high level of holiness in order to discern well. It does mean that our lives need to be fundamentally oriented toward God.

It also means that Ignatian discernment is about making choices between two or more good alternatives. Tomorrow morning, when you ask yourself "What should I do?" the options for the day do not include misleading your boss, retaliating for a slight, or hiding something from your spouse. You might not be full of magnanimity and generosity all the time, but your intention is to do the right thing, which means that you want what God wants for the day.

It follows that discernment won't steer us in directions that are unpleasant and alienating. It's not uncommon for Christians to think that the most difficult, challenging, and grimmest option is the one that God wants: *I need to spend my lunch break trying to be nice to that guy I can't stand. I should volunteer to give a talk even though I hate speaking in front of groups. I should quit my job and work in a soup kitchen.* This way of thinking has its roots in a certain kind of severe spirituality that greatly values austerity and sacrifice. A kind of heroic virtue can be seen as the ideal, giving rise to the feeling that to follow a path that is pleasing and satisfying to us is to settle for second best.

If we want more of God, he will point us in a direction that is consistent with our deepest desires. Our deepest desires are his deepest desires. Discernment leads to choices that make us more and more into the person we are meant to be. Our journey with God may take us to surprising places, but these will not be places that are repugnant to us or that alienate us from ourselves.

Another misconception is that discernment involves decoding secret messages. "God's will" is seen as a deep enigma shrouded in mystery. God scatters a bunch of hints and clues; discernment is about figuring out what they mean. Admittedly, discernment is often uncertain, but God doesn't enjoy hiding things from us and making decisions difficult. The hard work of discernment is sifting through our illusions and conflicting desires to find the way that truly satisfies us.

Discernment isn't about finding answers. It's about a deepening relationship with God. It's a journey together; it's more like dancing together than walking alone. This is the promise that discernment holds out: We can live in the Spirit. We can hear God. We can find what will give us greatest joy. We can attain what we really want.

2

What Is "God's Will"?

The purpose of discernment is to find "God's will." Ignatius himself said as much. What we're after, he wrote, is to "seek and find the divine will." But what does that mean? Does God have everything mapped out for us—a blueprint for our lives that we need to discover and conform to? Does God have one "correct" choice in mind for every important decision? In small decisions does he have a precise idea of how we should live every day? "God has a plan for you": It's a pretty common idea. God's will is something external to us; we have to figure out the plan and follow it.

But this is unlikely to be the case. For starters, logically, where do you stop? If God has one right answer for every question, you can't draw any line with God's plan on one side and our personal choice on the other. God must know which project you should work on tomorrow morning, what you should cook for dinner tonight, which errands to run, and which route you should take as you do them. He must know the music you should listen to and the best television programs to watch. The "one answer" principle quickly becomes untenable. It's also incompatible with the free will that God has given us. God gives us wide latitude and much room for discretion. He wishes us to freely choose to love. He doesn't coerce or limit us.

Another point: Most Christians, including most of the saints, don't get God's certain answer to the questions they ask. Sometimes they do. Christ appears to Paul in a blinding vision. God speaks to Augustine through a Scripture passage that the future saint reads at random. But these cases are the exceptions—presented as miracles—to God's intervention in the usual course of events. Far more common is uncertainty, even wandering in the darkness for a while. If discernment means finding the one right answer to every question, why is it so rare?

In fact, many things are good. The good is plural. God is abundant, not limiting. Most of our choices are among good, better, and best—not right and wrong.

WHAT IS GOD LIKE?

Our notions of what "God's will" means is rooted in what we think God is like. The totality of God is beyond our knowing. What we have are *images* of God—pictures in our minds that capture part of God's essence. These images are powerful, and they influence the way we think about choices. Growing up, most of us learned a simple image of God as the Boss who is in charge of everything (except when, mysteriously, he seemed not to be). There are variations on the Boss. Some bosses are stern judges enforcing the rules with punishments. Some are hard taskmasters, demanding much and upholding high standards. Some are benevolent, tolerating just about everything with a kindly smile.

As we go on in life other images of God usually appear, but the image of God-as-Boss is a powerful one, and some features of it can persist. We can continue to see God as somewhat separate from creation—overseeing the world from the corner office or the penthouse. We can see him as primarily the solver of problems. This causes us to see discernment as essentially a matter of solving a puzzle, with the lingering fear of making a mistake.

Ignatius's image of God was very different, and it shaped his whole understanding of the process of discerning God's "will." He developed this image in some detail at the end of the *Spiritual Exercises* in a series of meditations known as the Contemplation to Obtain the Love of God. It's actually several images of God.

Here's the first image:

> This is to reflect *how God dwells in creatures*: in the elements giving them existence, in the plants giving them life, in the animals conferring upon them sensation, in man bestowing understanding. So He dwells in me and gives me being, life, sensation, intelligence; and makes a temple of me, since I am created in the likeness and image of the Divine Majesty.

If you're looking for the heart of Ignatian spirituality, here it is. "God dwells in creatures," and "creatures" has the widest possible definition. God is present in all things. This is Paul's image of God: "For from him and through him and to him are all things" (Rom 11:36). Ignatius said that his friends "should practice the seeking of God's presence in all things, in their conversations, their walks, in all that they see, taste, hear, understand, in all their actions, since His Divine Majesty is truly in all things." The Jesuit theologian St. Robert Bellarmine went even further. "What various powers lie hidden in plants! What strange powers are found in stones," he said.

Some Christians are acutely sensitive to God's absence from the world. Ignatian spirituality emphasizes his presence. This brings God down to earth; "Christ is found in ten thousand places," said the Jesuit poet Gerard Manley Hopkins. It elevates earth to God; Hopkins also wrote, "the world is charged with the grandeur of God." "Nothing human is merely human," writes the theologian Ronald Modras. "No common labor is merely common. Classrooms, hospitals, and artists' studios are sacred spaces. No secular pursuit of science is merely secular." Everything that deepens our humanity deepens our knowledge of God.

The Ignatian God doesn't dwell in lonely splendor in the highest heavens. He doesn't even sit in the corner office. He's *here.*

The Contemplation continues:

> Consider how God *works and labors* for me in all creatures upon the face of the earth, that is, He conducts Himself as one who labors. Thus, in the heavens, the elements, the plants, the fruits, the cattle, etc., He gives being, conserves them, confers life and sensation.

Here Ignatius sees God as the worker—"one who labors." God the king, the judge, the merciful forgiver, the gift-giver, the unfathomable Other is also the creative power sustaining, healing, and perfecting the world. In the Ignatian view, something is always happening.

The creator God of Genesis is a worker. He doesn't create out of nothing; he brings order to chaos. Before he set to work, "the earth was a formless void and darkness covered the face of the deep" (Gn 1:2). Out of this unpromising raw material came the sun, the moon, and the stars; day and night; the land teeming with plants and animals; and, eventually, us. This is Ignatius's God—a God who never stops creating. He's at work now bringing order out of the chaos of our world. The Holy Spirit of God moves through this seething mass of passion, energy, conflict, and desire giving us culture, religion, art, science, and all the other elements of our familiar world.

This is why discernment is important. We have a role to play in this creative work. Most of it isn't glamorous work. "Smiting on an anvil, sawing a beam, whitewashing a wall, driving horses, sweeping, scouring, everything gives God some glory," writes Gerard Manley Hopkins. "To lift up the hands in prayer gives God glory, but a man with a dung fork in his hand, a woman with a slop pail, gives him glory too."

The Contemplation ends with a final vision of God as the infinitely generous, inexhaustible giver of gifts:

> To see how all that is good and *every gift descends from on high*. Thus, my limited power descends from the supreme and infinite power above—and similarly with justice, goodness, pity, mercy, etc.—as rays descend from the sun and waters from a fountain.

God dwells in all things; he works in all things; he makes us a gift of all things. He's like the sun, and his gifts are like the sunshine. The sun *is* sunshine. God *is* gift, and the sun always shines.

"What does it matter, all is grace," are the dying words of the lonely, forgotten, anonymous priest in the novel *The Diary of a Country Priest*. They echo the last words of St. Thérèse of Lisieux: "Grace is everywhere." The Spiritual Exercises end on this note—with a numinous vision of light and water, with all as grace, with gifts coming to us endlessly from God, who is Love itself.

A PERSONAL GOD

Ignatius emphasized one other aspect of God's character that's important for discernment. God is *personal*. He is very close to us. Ignatius imagines God looking on the world in all its splendor and suffering: "the happy and the sad, so many people aimless, despairing, hateful, and killing, so many undernourished, sick and dying, so many struggling with life and blind to any meaning. With God I can hear people laughing and cursing, some shouting and screaming, some praying, others cursing." God's answer to this spectacle is to say, "Let us work the redemption of the whole human race." The remedy is Jesus, who enters into it all. God enters into our suffering by sharing it. Jesus comes to heal and redeem. Jesus "does all this for me," Ignatius writes.

Friendship is a term often used in the Ignatian tradition to describe our relationship with God. Ignatius frequently urges us to speak to God intimately, "as one friend to another, making known his affairs to him, and seeking advice in them." Pope Francis often talks about Christ as our friend. "He is close to each one of you as a companion," the pope said. He is "a friend who knows how to help and understand you, who encourages you in difficult times and never abandons you. In prayer, in conversation with him, and in reading the Bible, you will discover that he is truly close. You will also learn to read God's signs in your life. He always speaks to us, also through the events of our time and our daily life."

The Jesuit spiritual director William A. Barry says that friendship is the purpose of creation. "God desires humans into existence for the sake of friendship," he writes. He says that developing a relationship with God is "analogous to the kind of friendship that develops over a long time between two people." He draws out the contrast between this friendship and conventional images of God. God our friend is not God the majestic, all-powerful, and distant ruler. It's not God as lawgiver and judge. As Father Barry's Irish mother put it, "God is better than he's made out to be."

A God who wants friendship with us, who's present in all things, who labors ceaselessly to save and heal the world, who pours out blessings like an endlessly flowing fountain—a God like this isn't an Engineer-in-Chief laying out a blueprint for everyone's life. Our job isn't to follow a set of divine instructions but rather to grow closer to a God who loves us and desires to be our friend. As we love him more, we will discern the right path. "Let the risen Jesus enter your life—welcome him as a friend," says Pope Francis. "Trust him, be confident that he is close to you, he is with you, and he will give you the peace you are looking for and the strength to live as he would have you do."

WHAT DO YOU REALLY WANT?

This brings discernment into clearer focus. Discernment is about loving and following God, not struggling to make the "right" decision. Our end is union with this God who loves us and who desires the best for us. Our decisions are the means to this end. As Ignatius put it, "I ought to do whatever I do, that it may help me for the end for which I am created." The Gospel story of Martha and Mary is about this very thing. When Jesus came to visit, Martha busied herself with the chores of hospitality while Mary sat with Jesus and listened to him. Jesus chided the busy Martha: "You are worried and distracted by many things; there is need of only one thing. Mary has chosen the better part" (Lk 10:41-42). The main thing in discernment—the one necessary thing—is to *love God first*.

If we love God first, it doesn't matter if the path we follow in life is circuitous, with frequent loops, retreats, and cul-de-sacs. It matters little if the decisions we make turn out very differently than expected. No one knew this better than St. Ignatius. He called himself "the pilgrim." In the tradition of pilgrimage, the journey itself is at least as important as the goal. His path in life was a meandering one, but Ignatius deeply believed that we can confidently walk along that path, finding the course that pleases God and brings us the deepest joy.

Notice the positive view of human nature that underlies this attitude. Ignatius was no Freudian. He knew nothing of libidos and ids and Oedipus complexes, and would have rejected the claim that they drive our behavior. He was no Calvinist; he didn't think that the human soul was so irreparably damaged by sin that it is incapable of knowing the good. He didn't view desires with suspicion as many religious people do. Ignatius loved desires. In the *Spiritual Exercises*, he continually says, "Pray for what I want." He believed that our deepest desires—what he called the "great desires"—are for loving union with God and others.

Thus we arrive at perhaps Ignatius's greatest insight in the matter of discernment. God placed these great desires in our hearts. Finding God's "will" means discovering what they are. This is what we *really* want. Ignatius believed that when we find what we really want, we find what God wants too.

Ignatius came upon this insight through his own experience of conversion. Through a process of reflection and discernment he came to understand that his deepest desire was to surrender himself completely to Christ and to go wherever Christ sent him. This desire had always been there. He had been restless and unhappy in his life as a military man and court official. When he recognized his deepest desires—when he discovered what he *really* wanted—he found peace and joy.

You might say that *of course* God wanted Ignatius to walk the difficult and demanding path of celibacy and poverty. That God wants *everyone* to do the hardest thing. But God doesn't work that way. Ignatius found the way of life best suited for *him*. If he had been a different person, it's entirely possible that a career of service to the king would have given him more happiness than a life as a priest. In fact, that must have been God's desire for any number of young men in sixteenth-century Spain. But it wasn't his desire for Ignatius, and it wasn't Ignatius's deepest desire for himself.

Finding what you really want doesn't mean "follow your bliss" or "do the work that makes you happy." The problem is that we don't know what will make us happy. Following our bliss frequently makes us miserable. We want many things, contradictory things—money and a balanced life; relationships and excitement; the esteem of others and the satisfactions of humble service. The hard work of discernment involves sorting through these desires and wants and passions and needs and discovering the kernel of authentic desire that God placed within us.

"LOVE GOD AND DO WHAT YOU WILL"

"God's will" isn't something external. It's internal. It's implanted in our hearts. Doing God's will isn't a matter of finding out some undiscovered item of "God's plan" and putting it into effect; it's more a matter of growing into the kind of person we're meant to be. It's the expression of the deepest truths of ourselves within the setting of a day-to-day relationship with God. The question to ask is, Is this action consistent with who I am and want to become?

We can answer this question with confidence if we sincerely love God and seek to follow in the footsteps of Christ. Here's the solution to the paradox of discernment. On the one hand, God cares about us and knows us intimately. We're supposed to follow him in everything, large and small. On the other hand, God has given us free will and reason. We're free to do what we want. These two principles seem to pull in opposite directions—but they are really two sides of one thing. If we love God, then what we most deeply want and what God wants are the same thing. Augustine made this point in his famous saying, "Love God and do what you will." If you truly love God, doing what you want will be doing what God wants.

It's simple—but not easy. The question "What do you really want?" is difficult to answer. We want many things. Many of
them aren't worth having. Many will make us miserable instead
of happy. Ignatius knew this very well. He developed an approach to discernment that helps us sift through our competing
desires. It's an approach based on learning to listen to what our
heart is saying.

3

The Language of the Heart

Discernment is about learning a new language. It's actually a language that we've heard all our lives—the feelings, moods, emotions, leadings, intuitions, and senses that constitute the affective part of our minds. Psychologists talk about the three parts of the mind: the *cognitive* (reason and other mental processes), the *conative* (the will), and the *affective* (feelings and emotions). All of these are involved in the choices we make, but the engine that drives the train is the affective power. The traditional word for it is "heart."

Ignatius's great discovery was that we can discern the right path by listening to the language of our hearts. Discernment is about noticing and interpreting those deep currents of feeling that shape what we want, which in turn influence what we do. By no means did Ignatius neglect reasoning and the other powers of the intellect. But he thought that the rivers of feeling and emotion are where God's leadings can most readily be found.

Ignatius didn't think this up. It was a discovery he made at a particular time in a particular place. Psychologists speak about "aha! moments," those occasions when a sudden flash of insight reveals the solution to a difficult problem. Francis of Assisi's aha! moment came when God told him to rebuild his church. Ignatius's moment came when he was lying in bed in recovering from grievous wounds suffered in battle.

THE DAYDREAMING SOLDIER

Ignatius Loyola's path to sainthood was unconventional to say
the least. As a young man he was a proud, headstrong courtier
and knight at the royal court of Navarre. The ladies liked him; his
rivals feared him. Once he was arrested for brawling in the street
(probably in a dispute over a woman), making him one of the
few saints with a police record. His macho world came tumbling
down in 1521 when he was seriously wounded in a battle. He
was carried back to his family's castle in northern Spain where
he endured two excruciating operations to repair his shattered
legs. It took him many months to recover, long months of idleness, plenty of time to reflect on his life. He harbored dreams of
returning to his previous life of knightly valor, but he probably
knew that those days were over. He was a thirty-year-old washed
up knight with two bad legs, living at home, being nursed back
to health by his sister-in-law. He was ready for something new.

When he asked for something to read he was given the only
two books in the house—a life of Christ and a life of the saints.
Ignatius was a Catholic like everyone else in his society, but he
was not particularly observant and certainly not pious. Nevertheless, the books stoked his active imagination. He imagined
what it would be like to be a knight in the service of Christ. He
was inspired by the stories of St. Francis and St. Dominic. They
were great saints, but Ignatius thought he could be an even *greater* saint than they were if he chose to be. It was the same with
stories of the life of Christ. Ignatius also spent a great deal of
time daydreaming about his previous life—the battlefield glory,
the amorous conquests, the rivalries at court, the camaraderie
of his friends. He whiled away the long days of recovery, lost in
these daydreams.

But Ignatius also had a knack for observing himself. He
observed himself daydreaming, and what he noticed was this:
dreams of romantic and military glory left him depressed; dreams

of following Christ left him excited and inspired. He realized that his surface feelings of angst and discontent, and of joy and delight, were pointing to deeper things. It dawned on him that God was speaking to him through his feelings. Years later, when he was head of the Jesuits and one of the most esteemed churchmen in the world, he described his aha! moment. He referred to himself in the third person:

> This succession of such diverse thoughts lasted for quite some time, and he always dwelt at length upon the thought that turned up, either of the worldly exploits he wished to perform or of these others of God that came to his imagination, until he tired of it and put it aside and turned to other matters.
>
> Yet there was this difference. When he was thinking of those things of the world, he took such delight in them, but afterwards, when he was tired and put them aside, he found himself dry and dissatisfied. But when he thought of going to Jerusalem barefoot, and of eating nothing but plain vegetables and of practicing all the other rigors that he saw in the saints, not only was he consoled when he had these thoughts but even after putting them aside he remained satisfied and joyful.
>
> He did not notice this, however; nor did he stop to ponder the distinction until the time when his eyes were opened a little, and he began to marvel at the difference and to reflect upon it, realizing from experience that some thoughts left him sad and others joyful. Little by little he came to recognize the difference between the spirits that were stirring, one from the devil, the other from God.

Ignatius realized that these feelings weren't just shifting moods that came and went in his enforced idleness. They had spiritual meaning. God was speaking through them. His fantasies represented two directions his life could take, and God was using his feelings to point him in the direction he wanted him to go. He realized that a life of dedication to Christ and his work was the life that would bring him joy and satisfaction.

Ignatius's experience of discernment on his sickbed opened his eyes a little. There was more to come. He followed the direction indicated by his feelings. When he recovered, he put on the clothes of a poor man, mounted a donkey, and journeyed across Spain as a pilgrim, seeking to go wherever God might lead. The road led to great things. People were drawn to him. A band of like-minded brothers formed around him; they became the Jesuits, which became the largest order in the Catholic Church, renowned for its missionary work and intellectual accomplishments—and for the spiritual perspective known as Ignatian spirituality.

Ignatius's insight into the spiritual meaning of his feelings eventually flowered into his system for discernment of spirits. It led to his rules for discernment that help us see the meaning of our inner lives. It led to forms of Ignatian prayer that build habits of reflective awareness of the continual presence of God in our lives.

WHAT KIND OF FEELINGS?

Feelings come in all shapes, sizes, and flavors. Some are intense but short-lived and not very meaningful. You might be powerfully moved by music—a Beethoven string quartet, a Bruce Springsteen concert—but these feelings don't last very long, and they seldom change you in any important way. Other feelings are more significant. They draw you into relationships (or pull you out of them). They affect how you spend your time. They affect your outlook on life, which affects how you treat other people and do your work. Some feelings change your commitments and affect your most cherished beliefs. Some of these deeper feelings are intense, but many aren't. They linger on the fringes of our consciousness; they hang around, until we realize what they mean and how important they are.

These are the affective states that discernment is concerned with—the ones that actually influence our behavior. These are the parts of the emotional life that have spiritual significance. They touch our sense of self—who we are and how we want to live. Some are triggered by external events. Others spring from our "inner world"—our imagination, dreams, prayers. Often we don't know where feelings come from. You wake up in the morning excited about the day ahead, or dreading it. You get anxious for no apparent reason. You feel confident about a plan that no one else thinks will work.

Ignatius believed that our affective life is an arena of spiritual conflict. The Holy Spirit is at work there, but so too are malign spirits, "the enemy of our human nature," as Ignatius called them. Discernment is concerned with determining the origin of these feelings and assessing their significance. A key question is: *Where* are these feelings leading us? Will they takes us in a positive, productive direction, or will they take us backward, or off on a tangent that distracts us from what's important? Many feelings are ambiguous. A good rule of thumb is to ask whether they move us toward a deeper connection with God and other people, or whether they tend to isolate us.

Ignatius classified spiritual feelings and emotions into two broad categories. One he called "consolation." This describes feelings that move us toward God and others. Consolation is any felt increase in faith, hope, and love. It is commonly experienced as feelings of peace, security, and joy. The other category is "desolation." It's the opposite of consolation—anything that takes us away from the love of God and others. We experience desolation as a troubled spirit: anxiety, restlessness, doubts, self-loathing, and dejection. One of the surest signs of desolation is spiritual lethargy. If you think that God is nowhere to be found, and that it's not worth the trouble to establish contact, you're probably in a state of desolation. Other signs of desolation are feelings of self-pity and meaninglessness. If you feel incompetent and your work seems pointless, desolation has settled on your soul.

We'll have a lot more to say about consolation and desolation later when we get into Ignatius's rules for discernment.

CONVERSION OF THE HEART

The true object of discernment is something deeper than emotions. The shorthand word for it is "heart." "Heart" does not mean the emotions (though it includes our emotions). It refers to our inner orientation, the core of our being, the things we love. This "heart" is what Jesus was referring to when he told us to store up treasures in heaven instead of on earth, "for where your treasure is, there your heart will be also" (Lk 12:34). This is the "heart" Jesus warned about when he said, "For out of the heart come evil intentions, murder, adultery, fornication, theft, false witness, slander" (Mt 15:19). Jesus observed that our heart can get untethered from what we say and do: "This people honors me with their lips, but their hearts are far from me" (Mt 15:8). When we don't have any enthusiasm for a project we say, "My heart isn't in it." The heart is what we really are. We're betraying our heart when we hurt people we love and do things that are contrary to our best idea of ourselves.

What we're after is a change of heart. We need to align our actions with our deepest desires. This is what happened to Ignatius. He underwent a profound conversion, but it was not a conversion of the intellect or will. Before his conversion he was an

orthodox Catholic who followed the religious practices expected of him. That was not what changed. His conversion involved
his deepest desires and commitments. His religious practice and
intellectual understanding deepened over time, but it was his
heart that was transformed.

Ignatius developed the Spiritual Exercises to bring about the
same kind of conversion of the heart in others. He wrote that
the purpose of the Exercises is "strengthening and supporting us
in the effort to respond ever more faithfully to the love of God."
Note what Ignatius did *not* say. He did not say that the Spiritual
Exercises are designed primarily to deepen our understanding or
to strengthen our will. He did not promise to explain spiritual
mysteries or enlighten our minds. We may emerge from the Exercises with enhanced intellectual understanding, but the goal is
a response of the heart to Christ's invitation to follow him and
be like him.

Something Pedro Arrupe said sums up what Ignatius had in
mind. Arrupe was superior general of the Jesuits from 1965 to
1983. By all accounts he was a lovable, enchanting man, deeply
spiritual, infectiously optimistic. He seems to have been one of
those rare characters who lights up the room, who makes you
feel like he's your best friend as soon as you shake his hand.
One of Arrupe's best-known quotes begins this way: "Nothing
is more practical than finding God, that is, than falling in love in
a quite absolute, final way." He continues:

> What you are in love with, what seizes your imagina-
> tion, will affect everything. It will decide what will get
> you out of bed in the morning, what you will do with
> your evenings, how you will spend your weekends, what
> you read, who you know, what breaks your heart, and
> what amazes you with joy and gratitude. Fall in love, stay
> in love, and it will decide everything.

There's no better description of the goal of discernment. It's about falling in love. It's about tapping into those deep currents of feeling that shape what we want, which in turn influence what we do. Understanding is important, and the will is vital, but what gets you out of bed in the morning is what you love. This is what discernment is about.

We often think about spiritual renewal as a matter of changing the way we think. This is a danger even in a book like this, which sets forth ideas, concepts, and principles to broaden our understanding of discernment. Understanding is important, but it's not the goal. We can understand many things without our knowledge affecting the way we live. The goal is a response of the heart, which truly changes the whole person.

WE CAN TRUST OUR EXPERIENCE

Most religions have codes and rules, things to avoid and things to believe. This is particularly true of Christianity, which has greatly valued creeds and doctrines and theology from almost its earliest times. Ignatian spirituality emphasizes the inner experience that gave rise to the creeds. The Ignatian way of discerning what is "of God" looks to our personal experience. Ignatius would have us experience God from the inside out, constantly discerning what leads us away from God as well as those things that bring us deeper into the divine life. Our Christian choices and decisions are often beyond the merely rational or reasonable. "The heart has its reasons of which the mind knows nothing," Pascal said.

Ignatius insisted that we can trust our personal experience. We know that our minds can perceive the ways of God; Ignatius insists that our hearts can too, more richly than our intellect can. Some object to this idea, pointing out that emotions are notoriously fickle and ambiguous. True—that's why Ignatius developed his rules for discernment. They may be fickle, but the feelings that stir our affective lives contain priceless knowledge of God, and they lead to the conversion of the heart which commits us zealously to the cause of Christ. After all, why *wouldn't* God be present in our everyday experiences? That's where we live our lives. Anxiety, peace, joy, irritation—these and the many other feelings we experience are signs. They say: look here. Something important is going on.

Note the essential optimism of Ignatius's view. Many Christians are fairly gloomy. They sense God's absence from the world more than his presence in it. They believe that our ability to perceive and respond to God is gravely impaired by sin, prone to error, unreliable. The godfather of this attitude is St. Augustine, who thought that grace was bestowed sparingly; humanity for him was a *massa damnata*—mostly destined to hell. Ignatius's view was very different. He believed that God was present in the world—"God is found in all things"—and that God bestows grace in abundance. One of the most vibrant ways that God is present to us is our personal experience. Ignatius knew this because it happened to him—a sinner who gave little thought to God for much of his life. He felt that if God would speak to him, he would speak to anybody.

Ignatius's method of discernment is suffused with this spirit of optimism. God is *here,* not out there. He's present in our everyday lives. We can connect with God by reflecting on our personal experience, which is reliable, not deceptive; meaningful, not inconsequential. Sometime this might seem too good to be true. But it is true. The Holy Spirit moves in our hearts, pointing the way.

4

Becoming Aware

To understand the language of the heart we first have to hear it. Discernment requires a finely tuned sensitivity to the inner life. Ignatius called this ability to notice the Spirit's presence a "spiritual sense." This isn't so easy. Most of us aren't used to finding God in our consciousness and memories. We look elsewhere for God.

That's the point of a well-known story about hearing God's voice that features the prophet Elijah. Elijah is told to go to the mountain and wait for the Lord to pass by. A strong wind comes, but the Lord isn't in the wind. Then there's an earthquake, but the Lord isn't in the earthquake. Then fire, but the Lord isn't there either. Finally, the Lord comes—in "the sound of sheer silence" (1 Kgs 19:12). Other translations call it "a gentle whisper," "a still small voice," "a whistling of a gentle air," "a light silent sound." The story implies that God speaks through internal spiritual movements more often than through external signs. We might occasionally find God's direction in wind, earthquake, and fire, but usually it requires concentrated attention and keen listening. The story also implies that God's presence is often a delicate thing, partially hidden, evanescent. It takes an acutely sensitive ear to hear something like silence. The passage doesn't say so, but we might imagine that it took Elijah some time to learn how to hear God this way. God was present on the mountain all along, but Elijah may have stood there a long time before he could hear the still small voice.

THE INDISPENSABLE PRAYER

Ignatius knew how hard it is for us to hear the language of the heart. It took him a while to discern the presence of God in his reverie and daydreams on his sickbed. Over the years he developed a method of paying attention to the subtle interior movements of God's Spirit through prayerful reflection on the events of the day. His method is known as the daily Examen. It is the cornerstone of Ignatian prayer and the foundation of Ignatian discernment.

There are many versions of the Examen, but the one used most often in the Ignatian tradition has five steps, which most people take more or less in order.

1. Give thanks.

Look at your day in a spirit of gratitude. Everything is a gift from God.

2. Pray for light.

Begin by asking God for the grace to pray, to see, and to understand.

3. Review the day.

Guided by the Holy Spirit, look back on your day. Pay attention to your experience. Look for God in it.

4. Look at what's wrong.

Face up to failures and shortcomings. Ask forgiveness for your faults. Ask God to show you ways to improve.

5. Resolution for the day to come.

What will you do today? Where do you need God today?

For Ignatius the Examen is the indispensable prayer. He insisted that Jesuits pray it twice a day, at noon and before retiring, even if they were too busy to pray in other ways. He taught the Examen at the beginning of the Spiritual Exercises; he thought that the habits of self-scrutiny and reflection that the Examen instilled were essential to completing the Exercises successfully.

It typically takes about fifteen or twenty minutes a day to pray the Examen, though you can take as long as you want; there's no time limit on this prayer. Most people pray it at the end of the day before retiring; some pray it in the morning. The whole prayer is conducted in the spirit of prayerful, discerning reflection. It banishes the abstract and relishes the concrete. It treats every moment of every day as a blessed time when God can appear. It's a way to find God in all things.

The heart of the Examen prayer is the review of the events of the previous twenty-four hours. This is where we become aware of the subtle (or not so subtle) movements of the Spirit that we look at in discernment. But first, let's look at the steps that lead up to the review of the day.

GRATITUDE AND LIGHT

The first step, Ignatius tells us, is to *"give thanks to God our Lord for the favors received."* We begin the Examen by consciously and deliberately adopting an outlook of thanksgiving. This is not just a pair of rose-colored glasses we wear to get through a tough time. It's the heart of prayer. It's a window into the deepest truth about ourselves—that we are in a relationship with a loving God who is generous beyond our imagining. Thanksgiving is the right response to what this loving God has done for us. It's the essence of our spiritual condition.

Gratitude was so important to Ignatius that he thought that *ingratitude* was the deadliest of sins. Out of all sins and evils, he

wrote, "ingratitude is one of the things most worthy of detesta-
tion." So much so, he continued, that ingratitude is "the cause,
beginning, and origin of all evils and sins." Ignatius was not given
to flowery rhetoric and hyperbole; he meant what he said—that
ingratitude is a mortal threat, greater perhaps than pride and lust
and envy and the other seven deadly sins. He saw gratitude as
a fundamental part of our relationship with God. Ingratitude is
something like willful blindness to the truth.

Gratitude leads to humility. If our spirits are filled with grateful thanks, we lift the burden of pride. Ignatius valued humility
very highly; it's the virtue we need the most if we are to discern
well. (More about this later.)

The second step is to pray for enlightenment to see our lives
through God's eyes. Jesus promised us that "the Spirit of truth
. . . will guide you to all truth" (Jn 16:13). At the beginning of the
Examen we ask the Holy Spirit to show us what we cannot see
ourselves. In the Examen we are relying on the human faculty
of memory to connect with God, but memory is fallible, unpre-
dictable, and sometimes muddled. We pray that the Holy Spirit
will use our flawed memories to yield trustworthy insights.

This is how Ignatius describes the second step of the Examen: *Ask for grace to know my sins and to rid myself of them.* We're
asking for three things: (1) grace; (2) to know; and (3) to be free.

"Grace" means "gift." We pray that God will give us the gift
to see through his eyes. Another way to put it is that we are pe-
titioning God to give us the gift of seeing his gifts.

We pray "to know." We want to see what has been hidden
and understand what has been murky. We want to become aware.

Finally, we pray to be free—"to rid myself" of my sins. Sin
in the Ignatian perspective includes the whole panoply of ideas,
dreams, desires, longings, and hungers that keep us from becoming the kind of people we were meant to be. In the second step
of the Examen we are praying to know what we really want.

A PRAYER OF MEMORY

The heart of the Examen is a review of the previous day. It's a prayer of memory. When asked how he prays, Pope Francis said, "Prayer for me is always a prayer full of memory, of recollection, even the memory of my own history or what the Lord has done in his church or in a particular parish." He continued: "I also know that the Lord remembers *me*. I can forget about him, but I know that he never, ever forgets me."

The Jesuit theologian Walter Burghardt said that prayer is "a long, loving look at the real." The Examen is about what *really* happened—not what might have happened, or what you wish had happened, or what might happen if things go right (or wrong). In the Examen, we're talking about being real in two senses. The first is the concrete reality of our everyday life. The second sense is "the reality beneath the reality." We're looking to find the spiritual reality that runs through our day. You summon the memories of the hours you have just lived and try to experience those events as you lived them. Yes, past events have shaped today's circumstances. Yes, you will eventually be making decisions that will shape your future. But at this moment in the daily Examen you are looking at what is.

We look at the real for a reason. This isn't a contemplative immersion into the wordless eternal NOW. We do it to discern the deeper truth about ourselves. We do the Examen to discover things: Where is God? How do I respond to him? What do I want most of all?

Here's what Ignatius said about the third step of the Examen:

The third point is to demand an account of my soul from the time of rising up to the present examination. I should go one hour after another, one period after another. The thoughts should be examined first, then the words, and finally the deeds.

The first part seems clear enough; Ignatius recommends going through the day in sequential order. The last sentence is puzzling: What did he mean by "the thoughts should be examined first, then the words, and finally the deeds"? Deeds, surprisingly, are last. They are less important than the "thoughts" and the "words." George Aschenbrenner, S.J., says that "thoughts" and "words" are best understood as referring to our emotions. He says, "It is here in the depths of our affectivity, so spontaneous, strong, and shadowy at times, that God moves us and deals with us most intimately."

This is what Ignatius learned on his sickbed; what he *felt* was more meaningful than what he *did*. We recall feelings more than actions to discern the presence of God. Ignatius says that we should pay particular attention to what he called consolation and desolation. They are feelings and moods that we have all the time. We find him in those times when we have felt happy, joyous, and at peace. We also find him in times of anxiety and sadness, because those are times when we need God.

WAYS TO REVIEW THE DAY

The Examen can be done in many ways. If you are led by the Holy Spirit when you pray the Examen, you will find your own way to pray it, and you are likely to pray it differently as time goes on. Here are some ideas about how you might do the review of the day, offered in the spirit of freedom and flexibility that Ignatius valued so much.

The first idea comes from Ignatius himself: go through the day in sequence—*one hour after another, one period after another.* Begin with how you felt when you woke up. (Think about the dreams you had during the night, if you can remember them.) Go through the events of the day one hour after another—the places you've been, the people you encountered, the work you did. As you play this home movie in your memory, note the feelings that arise. Strong feelings—positive and negative—usually point to something of importance. Let them surface, look at them, ask the Holy Spirit to show you what they are saying about God's presence in your life and your response to it. Also be attentive to weaker, subtler feelings. Sometimes we're barely aware of something important.

It's hard to tell in advance what will turn out to be significant in your Examen. Dennis Hamm, S.J., says that the Examen is "rummaging for God." Everyone has a junk drawer around the house—a drawer full of "stuff"—pens and pencils, keys, notepaper, business cards, receipts, small tools, and mysterious odds and ends. The drawer is everything that happened in the previous twenty-four hours. You're rummaging around in it, looking for the couple of things that are especially significant.

Here are a couple of ways to do the rummaging. You might take just one feeling and pray from it. It might be the strongest feeling you remember—a moment of anger or an intense feeling of satisfaction. It might be the predominant feeling of the day—a restlessness, a calm serenity, a mild funk. Or the feeling might be something small and fleeting, something you've forgotten that the Spirit brings to mind. Use this as a springboard for prayerful reflection. What does this mean? Where does it fit in?

You might try reviewing your day through the filter of your particular gifts. The infinitely generous Giver of gifts has equipped you with certain talents—the things you do especially well. What have you done with your gifts lately? You're a good listener. Did you listen to anybody today? You have a talent for organizing. What have you done lately to bring order out of chaos? You have creative gifts. What have you drawn or written or played lately?

You might pay special attention to your relationships. Instead of asking "how am *I* doing?" ask "how is the *relationship* doing?" "What is *really* going on this relationship?" Why is there distance between me and this person? Why have I found such delight in getting together with this friend? The rhythm of the Examen consists of questions like these: Why am I drawn to this? Why am I avoiding that? What's going on here? What do I *really* want?

In the review of the day, we are especially interested in our *response* to God. God is abundantly *active*. Jesus calls. We answer. The dynamic is like the call and response of a gospel choir. He invites us to join him—the same way he invited fishermen, tax collectors, sinners, and idle bystanders in the Gospel stories. We respond—eagerly or grudgingly, wholeheartedly or fitfully. The Examen is a way to keep track of the quality of our response.

FACE UP TO FAILURE

The fourth step of the Examen is to correct what's wrong. Ignatius describes the fourth step very briefly: "*The fourth point will be to ask pardon of God our Lord for my faults.*" The last word can also be translated as "sins." The word "sin" isn't very popular these days because of all the menacing associations that go along with "sin." It suggests sinners cowering before an angry God, and carries strong connotations of personal guilt.

There's another problem with "sin." It's usually understood to mean discrete acts that violate moral laws. That's true, but the "sin problem" is something deeper than angry outbursts, lies, and other sinful actions. The problem is that "I am the kind of person who lashes out at people who offend me and deceives people who love me." The bad behavior is a symptom of a deeper problem—the problem is *me*. The problem, as Joseph Tetlow,

S.J., put it, is "the fact that I am from a dysfunctional family, work in a dysfunctional job, am surrounded by neurotics, with whom I fit perfectly."

Sin is failure. We're intimately acquainted with failure, and it's very concrete. A pet project falls apart; we don't get the job; small children misbehave and adult children get into trouble; a friend cuts off contact; marriages collapse. Some of it's our responsibility, and some of it's not. The Examen helps us by clarifying things. We see where we are quick to excuse ourselves: gossip that's really character assassination, angry tirades under the guide of "venting." On the flip side, the Examen can show us where we mistakenly blame ourselves. We aren't responsible for other people's opinions and behavior. Sometimes you're wise, not lazy, to abandon a project that's draining your energy and isn't going anywhere.

Be careful not to let this step become morbid introspection. Remember: this is a *response* to something God has initiated. We are not pleading for mercy before a hanging judge. God has invited us to do this, and the Holy Spirit guides us every step of the way. Ignatius emphasized the reality of God's limitless love. He wrote in his diary that "God loves me more than I love myself." God *will* respond to us. Remember that the whole context of the Examen is love. God is a generous giver of gifts. He loves us more than we love ourselves, so we're free to look clearly at what's wrong and do what's necessary to set things right.

WHERE DO I NEED GOD?

The final step of the Examen is to resolve to act rightly in the day ahead. There are many things we *could* do; we'd like some more clarity about what we *should* do. The important thing is not to do any particular thing. It's "to move my heart toward what was pleasing to God."

One of Ignatius's most famous sayings is that "love ought to manifest itself in deeds rather than in words." The Examen looks at feelings and thoughts more than deeds, but in the end what you *do* matters most. Discernment is not an end in itself. It leads to deeds—to change, to work, to deeds of love. There's a chronic temptation to rest contentedly in the prayer and neglect the deeds. At the site of the Transfiguration the apostles wanted to build tents for Moses and Elijah to prolong the vision of glory that they enjoyed so much. At the Ascension the disciples mourned the departed Jesus until the angel came and rebuked them for gaping at the sky. There was work to be done!

Ignatius worded the fifth point of the Examen carefully: "*The fifth point will be to resolve to amend with the grace of God.*" You *resolve* to amend. The actual amending comes *with the grace of God*. It may not come easily; it may not come at all. The day to come will bring surprises. You may wind up doing something other than what you resolved to do. But you will do *something*.

WHY PRAY THIS WAY?

The Examen isn't like the prayer that most people are familiar with. It's not liturgical prayer, devotional prayer, or intercessory prayer. It's not prayer with Scripture. It's not contemplation or centering prayer. From the perspective of capital "P" Prayer, the Examen hardly looks like prayer at all. It's like ordinary life, considered in a certain way. So why exactly is this a good way to pray?

The theological answer is that God really is present in our world. He is *here*, not up *there*. This is the doctrine of the Incarnation—the belief that God has an intimate knowledge of our lives because he is human as well as divine. The Examen focuses on God as present in our human experience. This is part of our relationship with God. It's not the whole of it, but it's a vital part of it.

There are also some practical advantages to the Examen prayer. For starters, the Examen anchors our perception of God in daily human experience. The Examen reminds us that God is here once and for all. It assumes that God is present in our daily lives, and that his presence can be detected.

The Examen also answers the question, what do I pray about? Prayer can become routine—a time to think about our problems in the presence of the Lord. The Examen adds inexhaustible variety to prayer. To the question "What do I pray about?" it answers, "Everything that's happened to you in the last twenty-four hours." Does your everyday life feel like dreary same old, same old? The Examen shows it to be rich and meaningful. Every encounter, every challenge, every disappointment, every delight is a place where God can be found.

The Examen guards against a do-it-yourself attitude that can creep into the spiritual life. The idea that we can run our lives successfully by ourselves is the default stance in our self-empowering culture. This way of thinking can turn the spiritual life into an exercise in self-improvement, whereby we ask God to help us solve our problems. By contrast, the Examen is permeated with the spirit of gratitude and thanksgiving. It connects to a God who showers us with his gifts—the gift of life, of family and friends, of fruitful work. Even the ability to thank and praise God is one of God's gifts. By reminding us that we are not God, the Examen shatters the illusion that the world revolves around "me."

The Examen strips away illusions; it insists on honesty. It expels the temptation to put on a good face when we pray—to be someone who is kinder, more generous, more loving, "holier" than the person we really are. It's hard to maintain this façade when praying the Examen. As we review our day in the light of the Holy Spirit we are saying, "Here I am, Lord, warts and all."

CONTEMPLATION IN ACTION

An Examen can be done anywhere—stuck in traffic, eating lunch, walking to class, standing in line, in meetings. It becomes a habit; you begin to think reflectively, looking for the spiritual movements that are always present in the flow of daily events. The Examen slips the confines of a fifteen-minute prayer at a set time and becomes a "real time" Examen, a habitual way of looking at the world. This constant sensitivity to spiritual movements is the mindset of discernment.

Ignatius seems to have achieved this state of constant discerning awareness. Jerome Nadal, one of his closest friends, wrote that Ignatius was able "to see and contemplate in all things, actions, and conversations the presence of God and the love of spiritual things, to remain a contemplative in action." Becoming a "contemplative in action" is the Ignatian ideal. Contemplation and action have been viewed as two poles on the spiritual axis. Sometimes we pray; the rest of the time we work. Ignatius brought contemplation and action together. We can be people who are fully engaged in the work of Christ while being aware of God all the time.

This is how we "find God in all things." Finding God in all things doesn't mean that all things are divine. That's pantheism; Christians believe that the Creator is distinct from his creation. What the phrase means is that "all things" is where we find God. Our work, our relationships, the created world—all of it is the place where God is at work. We don't find him only in special places like church or in special times like morning prayer. The Examen cultivates a constant discerning awareness of God's presence at all times—even the busiest, most stressful, tedious times.

5

Great Desires and Disordered Attachments

Ignatius thought that the hardest work of discernment lies in identifying and overcoming "disordered attachments." Sometimes he called them "disordered affections." These are the things that we are in love with, the ends we pursue, the things we spend our money on and that take up our time. They are *affections*; we love them, crave them, cultivate and nurture them. We give them the benefit of the doubt. They are also *attachments*; they bind us, they come with us wherever we go, they take us places we don't want to go. They are the things we *must* have. The writer Chris Lowney calls the problem the "I-want-it-so-badly virus." He writes: "I so wanted to get to the top of the company, or to attract that attractive person, or to be rich, or to be recognized as important, or to have the best house, or to have a more exciting life. In fact, we sometimes delude ourselves into thinking that the object of our affection (the job, the car, the partner, the house) must be right for us precisely because we want it so badly."

Ignatius isn't talking about "affections" as we popularly understand them: a fondness for your grandmother or a liking for triple chocolate overload ice cream. He means the things that drive us, that get us out of bed in the morning—the things that influence our decisions and shape our lives. Almost any desire can become a disordered attachment: a desire to make money, a yearning to be admired, a drive to give the orders instead of following them, physical fitness, sexual pleasure, being in the know, being cool—all these things, and many others, can become the focus of our lives. The problem comes when these desires and affections become *disordered*—literally out of order. They crowd everything else out. There's nothing wrong with making money, but there's probably a lot wrong if you work all the time. There's nothing wrong with enjoying the admiration and praise of others, but something's out of whack if your decisions are driven by a craving for the limelight.

IGNATIAN INDIFFERENCE

To restore order, Ignatius suggests that we strive to achieve what he calls *indifference.* This means impartiality and objectivity, not a cold lack of concern. It means that we hold all of God's gifts reverently but also lightly, embracing them or letting them go depending on how they help us fulfill our vocation to love in the concrete circumstances of our lives.

The term *indifference* comes from Ignatius's First Principle and Foundation. We've already looked at the first part of it:

Man is created to praise, reverence, and serve God our Lord, and by this means to save his soul. The other things on the face of the earth are created for man to help him in attaining the end for which he is created. Hence, man is to make use of them in as far as they help him in the attainment of his end, and he must rid himself of them in as far as they prove a hindrance to him.

Here is the second part:

Therefore, *we must make ourselves indifferent to all created things,* as far we are allowed free choice and are not under any prohibition. Consequently, as far as we are concerned, we should not prefer health to sickness, riches to poverty, honor to dishonor, a long life to a short one. The same holds for all other things.

Our one desire and choice should be what is more conducive to the end for which we are created. (Emphasis added.)

Being "indifferent to all created things" means detachment. The all-encompassing goal is *freedom*. Indifference means that we are free from personal preferences, societal expectations, fears of poverty and loneliness, desires for fame and honor, and anything else that has a hold on us. It's a stance of openness to what God wants, which is what we most deeply want as well.

To make his point, Ignatius puts the matter in stark, even shocking, terms: *"We should not prefer health to sickness, riches to poverty, honor to dishonor, a long life to a short life."* You might say, "You've got to be kidding." Does Ignatius really mean that we shouldn't care whether we are sick or healthy, admired or despised? Not exactly—he's talking about the power of these desires. He's saying that we shouldn't allow concerns for our physical well-being, reputation, or financial security to control us. The problem comes when these things direct our lives.

You don't have to look far to find people whose lives are controlled by precisely the things Ignatius mentions. There are people who prefer health to sickness so much that their waking hours are filled with working out, healthy eating, and worries about environmental toxins, trans fats, and fructose. There are people who crave the esteem of others so much that they spend their days crafting sham perfect lives on Facebook. Many people work miserably in bad jobs to make money. Many people's lives are driven by passions for music, travel, food, sex, classic cars, celebrity news, and a million other hungers. The conventional wisdom tells us to "follow your bliss." In the Ignatian perspective, this is a risky strategy. It won't bring you happiness if your "bliss" is something other than what you want most deeply.

Ignatian freedom doesn't assume that sickness, poverty, disgrace, and an early death are the preferred outcomes. It means that you are as ready to choose a life of comfort as a life of hardship if that's what God wants. The free person's only desire is to become the person God meant them to be.

The Ignatian view of freedom means that everything in God's creation can be a way to God. It also means that you don't have to be afraid. That's what Ignatius told a Jesuit who feared for his spiritual well-being at the royal court where he worked. The court might be a snake pit of intrigue and dissipation, full of dangers, Ignatius wrote, but your calling is to be with these people and serve them. If you are faithful to your calling you have nothing to fear. "Christ himself will look after you," he wrote.

A THOUGHT EXPERIMENT ABOUT FREEDOM

In the *Spiritual Exercises*, Ignatius explores indifference and freedom in an exercise called the Three Classes of People. It's a thought experiment that imagines how people might react in a hypothetical situation. The point of the exercise isn't to identify good and bad choices. Everyone in the exercise is trying to do the right thing. The point is to invite us to think about what spiritual freedom really means.

Here's the exercise. These people have suddenly acquired a fortune of 10,000 ducats. While he was a student at the University of Paris, Ignatius could have lived for a year on about 50 ducats, so this is a fabulous fortune, beyond anyone's wildest dreams, like winning the Powerball lottery, or selling your money-losing start-up to Google for a billion dollars. The people are thrilled to get this money, but they are also Christians who understand that this fortune can be a fearful distraction and temptation. They know what Paul wrote in the First Letter to Timothy: "The love of money is a root of all kinds of evil" (6:10). The problem isn't money per se. It's *love* of money. The fortune can easily become a disordered attachment.

The first class of people talk about what to do—but all they do is talk:

> They would like to rid themselves of the attachment they have to the sum acquired in order to find peace in God our Lord and assure their salvation, but the hour of death comes, and they have not made use of any means.

The people in the second class try to free themselves from the attachment, but they attach strings to the situation under consideration. As Ignatius puts it:

> They wish to do so in such a way that they retain what they have acquired, so that God is to come to what they desire.

They decide what they want to do and then hope that God wants what they want. A person in the second class might set up a charitable foundation to give the money away with herself as the CEO. They are like Jesus's would-be followers in Luke's Gospel who make excuses when Jesus calls them: let me take care of some personal business first; then I'll come.

People in the third class free themselves of the attachment to the money by becoming indifferent to what happens:

> These want to rid themselves of the attachment, but they wish to do so in such a way that they desire neither to retain nor to relinquish the sum acquired. They seek only to will and not will as God our Lord inspires them,

and as seems better for the service and praise of the Divine Majesty.

This isn't just a matter of intention. "They will strive to conduct themselves as if every attachment to it had been broken":

> They will make efforts neither to want that, nor anything else, unless the service of God our Lord alone moves them to do so. As a result, the desire to be better able to serve God our Lord will be the cause of their accepting anything or relinquishing it.

Acting *as if* is an important point. People in the third class might still be attached to the money, but they will strive to act as if they weren't.

HOW FREE ARE YOU?

Ignatius probably wrote this exercise during the seven years he spent at the University of Paris from 1528 to 1535. He lived and worked with young men heading for brilliant careers. Think of Ignatius working today at Stanford University with grad students hoping to get rich in Silicon Valley, or at Harvard with young people heading for riches on Wall Street. Men like these could readily understand the temptations of a large fortune. But the Three Classes thought-experiment is about attachments, not money. Put yourself in the story. What are you strongly attached to? Perhaps it *is* money. Perhaps it's your career. Maybe it's your comfortable style of life. Maybe it's your leisure time, which you hoard jealously. You love this thing; it's hard to imagine going without it. But you know that this thing that you love so much has the potential to become a disordered attachment. That makes you uneasy. What do you do about this problem?

One option is to let it ride. You might talk to some people about it, pray about it, but in the end you let events unfold as they will. You don't make any changes in your style of life. You keep working in the job that pays so well even though you don't like it very much. You reason that God will let you know if this is a real problem; *then* you can make a change.

Another option is to bring God into the picture after you've decided what to do. You plunge into a new commitment—a project or graduate program or volunteer commitment—dedicating it to God without asking whether you should make the commitment in the first place.

If you choose one of these options, you would be acting like the people in the first and second classes. You wouldn't be morally wrong. Everyone in this exercise is trying to do the right thing, and the things they are attached to are good things honestly acquired. The exercise is about attachments, not judgments, and the point is that people in the first and second classes are controlled by their attachments. If you act like they do, you aren't free.

Your third choice is to strive to achieve freedom—indifference in Ignatian lingo. You do something that those in the other classes won't do: you could consider giving the thing up—give the money away, turn down the job, renounce the honor. You would be open to *all* options. This is what people in the third class do. They want only what God wants. This doesn't mean that your attraction to the thing goes away. To the contrary, you *know* that you are attracted to the money, honor, promotion, or whatever. It means that you want to make sure that this attraction doesn't become an attachment that controls your decision about what to do.

Let's be clear: The problem isn't the fortune; it's your *attraction* to the fortune—or to whatever you love so much. The exercise doesn't assume that God wants you to give the thing up. It may well be that God wants you to have it. Nor does the exercise imply that the attraction will go away. It may or may not. In fact we should assume that it won't. All our lives we will have many likes and dislikes, strong reactions to the things people do and don't do, passionate attraction to some possibilities and sharp revulsion to others. The challenge is to find a way to stand aside from these passions when we make decisions. The attitude we strive for is complete openness to whatever God wants.

CULTIVATING GREAT DESIRES

With the Three Classes exercise, we circle back to the question that lies at the heart of discernment: What do you really want? We want many things. Some point us in the right direction; some don't. Some are tightly focused; some are sprawling and amorphous. Some are simple (often deceptively so); some are intricate and mysterious. Some have an obsessive quality, dominating our thoughts and keeping us awake at nights; some are nagging voices at the back of our minds. The Three Classes exercise helps us begin to sort this out. If we're open to what God wants, we stand a good chance of discovering what we most deeply want.

The real subject of the exercise is desire. Ignatius loved desires. He thought that desire is the primary way God leads us to discover what we're meant to do. He called them "great desires"—the passions that touch us most deeply, that are integral to our sense of self. We're accustomed to thinking about growth in virtue as a matter of curbing our appetites and desires, as if our appetites only drive us toward the dark side. Some do, but we also desire God. Our deepest desires are for growth and change, and a fuller, deeper life. God speaks to us through these desires. They motivate us to become the people God created us to be. Discernment helps us identify these desires and follow them, to push aside disordered desires and get in touch with the deepest desires. We get in trouble not because we're captured by desires but because we're *not* captured by the deepest desires.

The Three Classes exercise is just an exercise. It doesn't really describe life as we live it. For one thing, reality is more complex than the exercise's static "classes" schema. We can be in all three classes at any one time—ignoring a problem in one area, negotiating with God in another, and achieving some degree of genuine freedom in yet another. Reality is also dynamic. Nobody falls completely into one class. We're always gaining ground in some areas and losing it in others.

This kind of freedom we need isn't easy to achieve, but we shouldn't make it out to be harder than it is. We can attain this kind of freedom because it's a gift from God. Ask for it. Ignatius constantly urges us to "ask for what you want." Pray St. Peter Faber's prayer for detachment:

> Cast from me every evil
> that stands in the way of my seeing you,
> hearing, tasting, savoring, and touching you;
> fearing and being mindful of you;
> knowing, trusting, loving, and possessing you;
> being conscious of your presence
>   and, as far as may be, enjoying you.
>
> This is what I ask for myself
> and earnestly desire from you. Amen.

6

Our Divided Hearts

When we become aware of our inner life, what do we find? We find God, but we find other movements and impulses and desires too. Nothing stays the same for very long. Our hearts are agitated, and the restlessness never seems to stop. This is true even for those who love God ardently.

This was Ignatius's experience while he was convalescing. His heart was pummeled by contrary impulses, some taking him toward God and some taking him away from God. This is why we need discernment; we need help sorting through these spiritual impulses, as Ignatius clearly saw. Ignatius's great insight was to see that the problem contains the seeds of its solution. These contrary impulses are meaningful. The upheaval in our spirits is not something to overcome; it's something to reflect on and learn from. When we learn how to interpret it, we will find the way forward.

The restlessness inside is a spiritual struggle. God is constantly inviting us into a deeper union with him, and other spirits are constantly pulling us away from him. Ignatius was a soldier, and so it was only natural that he would describe this inner struggle as a battle—spirits that move us toward God contend with those that move us away from him. Part of us wants to do the right thing; part of us doesn't. Sometimes we experience this struggle as mild pushing and shoving. Sometimes it's fierce combat. This spiritual struggle throws up a maelstrom of feelings, thoughts, and impulses that are the raw material for discernment.

GOOD AND EVIL SPIRITS

Ignatian discernment is a discernment of "spirits." Ignatius speaks of "the good spirit" and "the evil spirit." What exactly does he mean by this?

Ignatius made a distinction between God himself and "the good spirit," or "the good angel." A distinction between God's work and the action of good angels was a common one in medieval theology. When an experience touches our thoughts and senses, it is the work of the good angel. When something touches the soul directly, it is the work of God without an angel intermediary. This distinction isn't common today, and it doesn't have much practical importance. For our purposes, it's sufficient to take "the good spirit" as meaning God himself—the Holy Spirit.

"The evil spirit" is another matter. Ignatius calls this entity "the enemy," "our enemy," "the enemy of our progress and eternal salvation," and, often, "the enemy of our human nature." There's no doubt that he meant Satan, an evil spiritual person as real as the Holy Spirit, who "prowls about the world seeking the ruin of souls," as an old Catholic prayer puts it. Jesus believed in evil spirits, as did the writers of the Old Testament before him and most Christians after him, up until modern times. Today people are all over the map on the question of evil spirits. Some see demons at work everywhere. Some dismiss talk of devils (and angels) as superstitious nonsense. But only rigidly doctrinaire materialists deny the reality of malevolent spiritual powers in the world. As one theologian put it, "I can understand people who do not believe in God, but the fact that there are people who don't believe in the devil is beyond my comprehension."

Ignatius wrote with the intellectual framework of the sixteenth century in the language of his times. Satan got direct credit for things that we look at differently now. We know about mental illness and psychopathology, and we have a more acute understanding of the ways early childhood experiences and corrupt social systems can wound and disfigure human hearts. But this hardly explains the breadth and depth of the evil in the world. It doesn't explain the stubbornness of our hearts. We all know what Paul was talking about when he wrote: "I do not understand my own actions. For I do not do what I want, but I do the very thing I hate" (Rom 7:15).

With the gift of free will comes the capacity to choose good or evil. Most of the misery in the world stems from free human choices. We've all felt the impulse to choose something other than the good. Jesus taught us to pray "Thy Kingdom come, Thy will be done." Sometimes we live that prayer, and other times we simply want what we want without caring about God. There are parts of our personality that lead us to life and parts of ourselves that want us spiritually dead. That's our problem. Ignatius's great insight was to see that it's an opportunity as well.

THE TWO STANDARDS

The tumult inside is caused by contending spiritual forces each calling for our allegiance. We have to choose sides, and we have to understand the way each side issues its invitation.

The Two Standards, one of Ignatius's most powerful meditations in the *Spiritual Exercises*, is about choosing sides. He asks us to imagine two armies gathered around standards, or battle flags. One army is led by Satan, "the deadly enemy of our human nature," seated on a great throne of fire and smoke. Satan sends demons to all the ends of the earth with instructions to lead humans to ruin through desire for riches, honor, and pride. The second host is led by Christ, who sends his disciples out into the world to invite people to a life of poverty, rejection, and humility. The point of the meditation is that two masters with two very different value systems are vying for our allegiance, and you have to choose one or the other. If you're put off by the martial imagery, imagine some other scene where you have to make a big choice between two very different cultures. Sing the line from the Bob Dylan song, "It may be the devil or it may be the Lord, but you're gonna have to serve somebody."

A couple of details in the meditation are very interesting. Satan's standard is placed in "the vast plain about Babylon." Christ stands "in a lowly place in a great plain about the region of Jerusalem." The contest between Christ and Satan takes place in this world, not in some spiritual realm. The power of evil is centered on earth, not in hell, and God's kingdom is in this world, not in heaven. It's also noteworthy that both Christ and Satan work through agents. Satan sends out demons; Christ works through apostles, disciples, and other emissaries. Another detail: no part of the earth is left out. "No province, no place, no state of life, no individual is overlooked," says Satan. You don't get a pass if you're a priest or nun, come from a religious family, or live in a nation with a strong Christian culture. Everybody's in this.

Note what Ignatius says about the *tactics* of Christ and Satan. The exercise describes a spiritual progression; one thing leads to another.

Here's how Satan instructs his minions. Ignatius writes:

Consider the address [Satan] makes to them, how he goads them on to lay snares for men and bind them with chains.

First they are to tempt them to covet riches (as Satan himself is accustomed to do in most cases) that they may the more easily attain the empty honors of this world, and then come to overweening pride.

The first step, then, will be riches, the second honor, the third pride. From these three steps the evil one leads to all other vices.

It all begins with riches. It's the first step on a downward slope that ends with overweening pride.

Christ has a different set of instructions for his angels:

> Consider the address which Christ our Lord makes to all His servants and friends whom He sends on this enterprise, recommending to them to seek to help all, first by attracting them to the highest spiritual poverty, and should it please the Divine Majesty, and should He deign to choose them for it, even to actual poverty. Secondly, they should lead them to a desire for insults and contempt, for from these springs humility.
>
> Hence, there will be three steps: the first, poverty as opposed to riches; the second, insults or contempt as opposed to the honor of this world; the third, humility as opposed to pride. From these three steps, let them lead men to all other virtues.

The progression is the mirror image of Satan's. Poverty leads to humility and all the other virtues.

Neither Christ nor Satan present good or evil in their most obvious forms. Satan doesn't work through hatred, anger, jealousy, and the other usual suspects; he tempts us to riches and honor. These are not evil things in themselves; they can even be good. The same is true for Christ's program. He doesn't invite his followers to lives of kindness, mercy, and love. He offers poverty, obscurity, and humility. These aren't necessarily bad things, but they're not very attractive either. In fact, they can be quite undesirable. It's a nuanced picture: an offer from Satan that seems rather desirable; an invitation from Christ that's somewhat distasteful.

The first steps of both movements have to do with wealth and possessions. Ignatius was repeating Scripture's clear message about riches: "You cannot serve God and wealth" (Mt 6:24).

Time and again, Jesus says that riches are among the deadliest spiritual dangers. His disciples were shocked when he said
that it's easier for a camel to pass through a needle's eye than
it is for a rich man to get to heaven. Pious Jews thought that
wealth was a sign of God's favor. Jesus thought pretty much the
opposite: wealth separates us from God. The Two Standards exercise shows us why. Satan's plan begins with riches. "Riches" is
the "stuff" of the world—money, of course, but also the things
money can buy: homes, cars, time shares, vintage wine, fine
food, and assorted bling. It also includes intangible goods like
our skills, reputations, status. This stuff is just stuff, neither good
nor bad, until we assign meaning to it. If we view riches as very
important—the source of our security, the focus of our efforts,
the stuff that makes us who we are—we'll seek more of it. And
more. And more.

The problem isn't this stuff; it's the *longing* for the stuff. If
riches make you who you are, you'll want more of them, which
really means that you want more of yourself. Pretty soon, all
you care about is *me*. It's a progression, and the end is monstrous
pride. The Jesuit Joseph Tetlow puts it neatly. At first you say,
"Look at all this stuff I have." Then you say, "Look at me. I have
all this stuff." Finally, you say, "Look at ME."

By contrast, the endpoint of Christ's program is humility.
Humility isn't self-abasement. It doesn't mean that you hold
your tongue, never make a fuss, sit in the corner, and think that
everyone is better than you. "Humility consists in being precisely
the person you actually are before God," wrote Thomas Merton.
The truth is that world is full of other people with rights and
needs and unique gifts and weaknesses. It's a web, a network full
of ceaseless activity. You have a part to play in this great drama of
life, and it's not the starring role. The idea that you're the center
of things is an illusion. That's the way things really are.

The Two Standards exercise fills in something of the spiritual reality of what's going on inside us. Discernment is about

making choices in a dynamic context of spiritual struggle. Spirits jostle for influence and attention. Most of the choices we make have to do with a struggle between pride and humility. The content of it involves "riches" material and immaterial—our possessions, our talents and skills, our dreams and ambitions, the way others see us, the way we see ourselves.

We must decide what we value most highly. What do you really want? It's time to look at Ignatian discernment in detail.

7

Consolation and Desolation

Ignatian discernment is concerned with the affective states that Ignatius called consolation and desolation. These are old-fashioned words that seem puzzling to many today, but it's better to explain them than to replace them with more familiar words. Consolation and desolation describe familiar experiences, but it's easy to misinterpret what they mean.

Generally speaking, consolation is associated with positive feelings and desolation is associated with negative ones. When you're in a state of consolation you are likely to be feeling peaceful, energetic, and joyful. In desolation you feel anxious, depressed, and alienated. But consolation and desolation are not simply feeling good and feeling bad. They are *spiritual* states; they're about moving toward God and moving away from him.

You might feel disappointed, even crushed, when you don't get the promotion you've been hoping for, but this is not necessarily desolation. It's desolation if you draw negative and hostile conclusions from the experience—that you're incompetent, for example, or that your bosses are out to get you. Otherwise, it's simply a feeling of disappointment that has no special spiritual significance. You might feel great serenity as you sit on the boardwalk and watch the sun rise over the ocean, but this isn't necessarily consolation. It becomes consolation if the sight moves you to gratitude to God for the beauty of creation and the blessings of your life. Sometimes the spiritual state is almost the opposite of the surface feelings. You might experience a deep confidence and hope as you tackle a difficult project, even if you wish you didn't have to do it. You're experiencing consolation, even if you're not especially "happy."

The same idea can give rise to either consolation or desolation, depending on where it leads. Say you're in a group at work looking at a disappointing situation—bad sales numbers, for example, or a project that's in deep trouble. Some people are dejected about it, and look for someone to blame. Others are hopeful and eager to do something to help. You might reach the limits of your patience or talent or understanding and fall into depressed desolation. But seeing one's personal limitations can just as well lead to consolation. Ignatius once wrote that "The more I see myself, the more I see the whole of myself as [an] obstacle to God's work. This consideration brings me the greatest and sweetest consolation, because I realize that God in his loveliness works so many good things through me."

The important thing is not the events or circumstances but our reaction to them. If someone tells you, "God has shown me what a sinner I am; he's punishing me; I'm sad and depressed," you can be sure that God didn't show him that. Satan did. St. Peter Faber, one of the first Jesuits, wrote, "The Holy Spirit, even if he scolds, scolds sweetly."

It can be difficult to distinguish between surface emotions and deep spiritual movements. It can be confusing when the emotion says one thing and the movement another. We have to develop a sense for this. It helps greatly to have the help of an experienced spiritual adviser. Ignatius assumes that we are not trying to do this alone. It's no surprise that the Ignatian spiritual tradition places great emphasis on the importance of spiritual direction.

CONSOLATION

Ignatius defines spiritual consolation in one of the rules for discernment of spirits. It's actually more of a description than a definition—a series of examples by which consolation can be noticed. It's worth reading the whole thing:

> I call it consolation when an interior movement is aroused in the soul by which it is inflamed with love of its Creator and Lord, and as a consequence, can love no creature on the face of the earth for its own sake, but only in the Creator of them all. It is likewise consolation when one sheds tears that move to the love of God, whether it be because of sorrow for sins, or because of the sufferings of Christ our Lord, or for any other reason that is immediately directed to the praise and service of God. Finally, I call consolation every increase of faith, hope, and love, and all interior joy that invites and attracts to what is heavenly and to the salvation of one's soul by filling it with peace and quiet in its Creator and Lord.

Consolation is *"an interior movement,"* a lifting of the heart "to what is heavenly." But it also can be seen *externally*, in "tears" and other physical manifestations. The essence of consolation is loving the things on the earth, not for their own sake, but through God and for God. This is the meaning of "finding God in all things." Touched by the love of God, we find him everywhere. All things speak of God; all things can lift the heart to what is heavenly. Consolation comes when we follow the greatest commandment: "You shall love the Lord your God with all your heart, and with all your soul, and with all your strength, and with all your mind; and your neighbor as yourself" (Lk 10:27).

We have to distinguish between sensory consolations and those which come beyond the senses, deep in our hearts. The two are related. People who have fallen deeply in love will experience great passion and desire for each other. They will have feelings of happiness and euphoria. These feelings support and even deepen the lovers' bond. At the same time, we shouldn't work too hard to separate spiritual and "nonspiritual" consolation. They usually go together. We are creatures of spirit and flesh; we experience consolation in our bodies as well as our hearts.

Some people downplay the emotional side of consolation. They remind lovers that the joy and fervor of falling in love will pass, the honeymoon will soon be over, and the "real work" of a relationship will begin. Spiritual advisers will sometimes tell people not to seek out spiritual experiences because true conversion is a matter of the will and action, not feelings. The Ignatian tradition counsels otherwise; it welcomes passion, tenderness, excitement, fervor, enthusiasm, and other expressions of joy. We're to seek them out. Ignatius told Francis Borgia that "without these consolations all our thoughts, words, and actions are tainted, cold, and disordered." He continued, "We ask for them so that with them we may become pure, warm, and upright."

DESOLATION

Here is how Ignatius describes spiritual desolation:

> I call desolation what is entirely the opposite of what is
> described in the third rule, as darkness of soul, turmoil of
> spirit, inclination to what is low and earthly, restlessness
> rising from many disturbances and temptations which

lead to want of faith, want of hope, want of love. The soul is wholly slothful, tepid, sad, and separated, as it were, from its Creator and Lord. For just as consolation is the opposite of desolation, so the thoughts that spring from consolation are the opposite of those that spring from desolation.

In desolation we're afflicted with things we'd ordinarily like to get rid of—darkness, restlessness, turmoil, sadness. But there's a part of desolation that's attractive. This is the *"inclination to what is low and earthly."* Consolation is the attraction to heavenly things; desolation is attraction to worldly things. In discerning spirits we ask *where* the feeling is going—toward God or away from him. Desolation leads away from God. We want things for themselves, not because we find God in them. This is the essence of desolation. Our appetite for God is dying.

Desolation can be a very pleasant state. We can happily hunger for money, success, and entertainment, not giving a thought to God and to the work that will make us truly happy. In his autobiography, Ignatius recounts several instances where fascination with spiritual experiences distracted him from his responsibilities. These "false consolations" are actually forms of desolation. Ignatius devotes considerable attention to them in his rules for discernment of spirits.

Usually, though, desolation is experienced as a disagreeable condition. Darkness descends on the mind. Judgment is skewed; ordinary human situations involving both joys and sorrows, the sweet and the sour, are perceived as entirely hostile and hopeless. The soul becomes *wholly* slothful, tepid, and sad. Ignatius's description of desolation has two parts—the forms of desolation and the "thoughts" that arise from them. It's the thoughts that get us into real trouble: there's no hope, I'm a bad person, I can't pray, I can't do this, I'm a failure.

HOW THE SPIRITS USE
CONSOLATION AND DESOLATION

You might think that discernment looks like a fairly simple affair: the good spirit brings consolation; the evil spirit brings desolation. Once we identify spiritual states of consolation and desolation, we know what spirit is involved. "It would be pretty to think so," to quote Ernest Hemingway. It's not so simple.

A basic principle of discernment—and one of the most important—is that good spirits and evil spirits operate differently according to our fundamental spiritual condition. For someone who is regressing spiritually, the evil spirit will reinforce this condition by making evil appear to be good. The good spirit will do the opposite. It will stir up unpleasant feelings, raise doubts, sting the conscience to encourage the person to change course. The spirits operate in the opposite way in someone who is moving toward God. The evil spirit attempts to knock us off course by harassing us with anxiety, sadness, and doubts. The good spirit reinforces our direction by giving feelings of peace, assurance, and joy.

Ignatius explains how this works for the person in spiritual trouble:

> In the case of those who go from one mortal sin to another, the enemy is ordinarily accustomed to propose apparent pleasures. He fills their imagination with sensual delights and gratifications, the more readily to keep them in their vices and increase the number of their sins. With such persons the good spirit uses a method which is the reverse of the above. Making use of the light of reason, he will rouse the sting of conscience and fill them with remorse.

The evil spirit works on the *imagination*. The life of sin is a life full of "apparent pleasures"—illusions, dreams, counterfeit versions of real joys, false consolations. If the person's energy for sin wanes, the evil spirit will stoke the fire with a new burst of fanciful visions. The person in spiritual trouble is leading an imaginary life. To counteract these illusions, the good spirit will work in the person's conscience through the rational powers of judgment. Illusions are challenged. Are you really happy living this way? Why are you hurting people you love? These thoughts are troublesome and unpleasant; they "sting" the conscience and "fill them with remorse." The good spirit's work will feel like desolation; the evil spirit's apparent pleasures will feel like consolation.

For the spiritually maturing person, it's the other way around. For them:

> It is characteristic of the evil spirit to harass with anxi
> ety, to afflict with sadness, to raise obstacles backed by
> fallacious reasonings that disturb the soul. Thus he seeks
> to prevent the soul from advancing. It is characteristic of
> the good spirit, however, to give courage and strength,
> consolations, tears, inspirations, and peace. This He does
> by making all easy, by removing all obstacles so that the
> soul goes forward in doing good.

The evil spirit afflicts with *sadness*. This is sadness of the spirit, something Ignatius described in a letter: "We find ourselves sad without knowing why. We cannot pray with devotion, nor contemplate, nor even speak or hear of the things of God." The evil one harasses with anxiety. Interestingly, the evil spirit raises obstacles *"backed by fallacious reasonings."* For the spiritually regressing person, it was the good spirit that used logic and reason to undermine the illusions of a sinful life. Here it's the evil one who uses reason. We've all experienced it. You feel led to take some step toward greater devotion and more generous service and immediately a host of obstacles will come to mind. *That's too extreme. My family won't like it. This isn't the time to make new commitments. It won't work. It's too complicated.* "The logic is perfect," says the Jesuit spiritual director Anthony de Mello. "The devil has a PhD in logic."

As de Mello implies, the work of the evil spirit is subtle. Its goal isn't to destroy our faith; that would be easy to spot and reject. Rather it's a more modest goal, "to prevent the soul from advancing." To that end it sows doubts, speaking gently, reasonably. In a famous passage in his *Confessions,* St. Augustine describes the hesitations he felt as he stood at the brink of conversion:

> I was held back by mere trifles, the most paltry inanities, all my old attachments. They plucked at my garment of flesh and whispered: "Are you going to dismiss us? From this moment we shall never be with you again, for ever and ever. From this moment you will never again be allowed to do this thing or that, for evermore."
>
> They no longer barred my way, blatantly contradictory, but their mutterings seemed to reach me from behind, as though they were stealthily plucking at my back, trying to make me turn my head when I wanted to go forward. Yet, in my state of indecision, they kept me from tearing myself away, from shaking myself free of them and leaping across the barrier to the other side, where you were calling me. Habit was too strong for me when it asked, "Do you think you can live without these things?"

To counteract the doubts and fears sowed by the evil spirit, the good spirit gives strength and courage. It sends consolations, assurances that God is here and that all will be well. The evil spirit uses the sinner's imagination to make a bad life seem attractive. For the spiritually maturing person, the good spirit uses the imagination to bolster courage and reinforce progress. God sent a literal vision to St. Augustine to spur him on to conversion. The good spirit appeared personified as Continence, surrounded by a crowd of ordinary people who loved God:

> She was smiling at me but with a challenging smile, as though to say, Can you not do what these men have done? These women? Could any of them achieve it by their own strength, without the Lord their God? He it was, the Lord their God, who granted me to them. Why try to stand by yourself, only to lose your footing? Cast yourself on him and do not be afraid.

With the spirit's tender smile and gentle encouragement, Augustine was able to overcome his fears and surrender to God.

THE RULES FOR DISCERNMENT

These descriptions of consolation and desolation, and of the way good and evil spirits use them, are the first four of twenty-two "rules for the discernment of spirits" appended to the end of the *Spiritual Exercises*.

We shouldn't take the term "rules" too literally. They are more like guidelines and good advice based on extensive observation rather than rules that describe how things work all the time. Ignatius says that his rules help us interpret spiritual movements "to some extent." He's careful to say that he is describing the ways spirits "ordinarily" behave. He recognizes that we only partially understand the workings of the spiritual realm. Real life is more complicated than any generalizations we can make about it. People are mixtures of flaws and strengths. We are making progress in some areas and sliding backward in others. The spirits operate in different ways in the same person and at the same time.

Nevertheless, the rules for discernment bring clarity to this jumbled picture. They cover a lot of ground. The first set of rules, fourteen of them, have to do with dealing with desolation. The second set, eight rules, are aimed at identifying "false consolations," those feelings of well-being and peace that are actually the work of the enemy. Right off the bat Ignatius is making two very important points: we are continually afflicted with desolation, and we need a great deal of help to resist and overcome it. What's more, not all consolation is from the good spirit. The evil spirit uses it too, and we need to be alert to the ways it can mislead and confuse us.

Let's look at the first set of rules—those dealing with desolation.

8

How to Thwart Desolation

The Spiritual Exercises are divided into sections that Ignatius called "weeks." These are stages of a person's progress through the retreat rather than designations of time. Ignatius says that the first set of rules for discernment are associated with the "first week" of the Spiritual Exercises. For those making progress in the spiritual life, desolation is a tool of the evil one. Our first task in discernment is learning how to deal with discouragement, self-loathing, alienation, and the other baleful feelings that can tear us down.

DON'T CHANGE ANYTHING

The first rule is to remain steadfast in your commitments and habits when you are in a time of desolation. Don't make big changes. Thomas Green, a renowned Jesuit author and spiritual director, says that we can avoid ninety percent of the unhappiness in our lives if we adhere to this simple principle.

Here's the rule as Ignatius wrote it:

Rule 5. In the time of desolation we should never make any change, but remain firm and constant in the resolution and decision which guided us the day before the desolation, or in the decision to which we adhered in the preceding consolation. *For just as in consolation the good spirit guides and counsels us, so in desolation the evil spirit guides and counsels. Following his counsels we can never find the way to a right decision.* (Emphasis added.)

Don't do anything now; go sleep on it. Sensible advice, yet it's often ignored. When we're hurting, our impulse is to act. You want to do *something* to make the bad feelings go away. Quit the job. Move away. Teach the kid a lesson. Dump the girlfriend or boyfriend (or, if you're the one who got dumped, find another one as quickly as possible). Sometimes a change is needed, but desolation is the worst possible time to figure out what it should be. Wait until the emotional storms pass; *then* decide whether anything needs to change.

We ignore this counsel for another reason too. Christians who are seeking a deeper spiritual life often assume that God is trying to tell them something when desolation comes. Restlessness, anxiety, discouragement, and the other signs of desolation are seen as symptoms of a problem that needs to be fixed. "I'm miserable; I can't pray; God seems far away—God must be sending me a message." No—Satan is sending the message. Ignatius explains why: *"In desolation the evil spirit guides and counsels."* God never sends desolation. He may permit it, but he's never the author of it. It's a big mistake to listen to the malign and destructive ideas that enemy suggests in desolation. *Following his counsels we can never find the way to a right decision.*

We're inclined to think of desolation as an aberration of some kind, that peace and joy and satisfaction are the normal state of affairs, that desolation is a nasty interruption of the right order of things. Ignatius saw desolation as normal. He viewed the spiritual life as a cyclical affair. Anxiety and contentment, joy and sorrow, peace and turmoil come and go. These feelings are produced by the ceaseless deep down spiritual struggle in our divided hearts, much of which takes place beyond our consciousness. Ignatius says, don't be upended by this. Sit tight and wait for the feelings to change.

COUNTERACTING DESOLATION

We know what *not* to do—don't make any changes in desolation. But is there anything positive we can do to work against desolation? That's the subject of the next three rules.

Two of them say that we should do the *opposite* of what the enemy is saying.

Rule 6. Though in desolation we must never change our former resolutions, it will be very advantageous to intensify our activity against the desolation. *We can insist more upon prayer, upon meditation, and on much examination of ourselves.* We can make an effort in a suitable way to do some penance.

Rule 8. When one is in desolation, he should strive to *persevere in patience.* This reacts against the vexations that have overtaken him. Let him consider, too, that consolation will soon return, and in the meantime he must diligently use the means against desolation which have been given in the sixth rule. (Emphasis added.)

In desolation the enemy seeks to turn us away from a healthy spiritual life. Often this takes the form of spiritual lethargy. We can't rouse ourselves to pray. Mass, the sacraments, and other spiritual practices seem tiresome and pointless. We sit and do nothing except daydream about what might be or might have been. Sometimes the attack comes in the form of restlessness and anxiety. We're too busy to pray. There's too much to be done in the world—good things, constructive things. We can't waste our time navel gazing.

Ignatius counsels both the lethargic one and the restless one to make a renewed commitment to the ordinary practices of the spiritual life—prayer and meditation, reading Scripture, self-examination. He makes mention of doing some penance—acts of self-denial that symbolically curb our appetites and remind us that God supplies everything we need. The point is to fight desolation in concrete ways.

The other way of fighting desolation is to master our thoughts.

> **Rule 7.** When one is in desolation, he should be mindful that God has left him to his natural powers to resist the different agitations and temptations of the enemy in order to try him. *He can resist with the help of God*, which always remains, though he may not clearly perceive it. For though God has taken from him the abundance of fervor and overflowing love and the intensity of His favors, nevertheless, he has sufficient grace for eternal salvation. (Emphasis added.)

In desolation our thoughts get scrambled. *I'm alone. God has departed on a long vacation. It's up to me to do something, and I don't have any idea what to do.* Ignatius reminds us that God is always there for us, even when we don't feel a divine presence. What desolation takes away is the "abundance" of fervor and love and divine blessing. Love always remains. The coal will always be glowing; perhaps it's covered with ashes; perhaps you can barely feel the heat. But it's there. No matter how bad you feel, people in desolation have "sufficient grace for eternal salvation."

WHY DOES GOD PERMIT DESOLATION?

Desolation is a normal occurrence, but why? Why should the Lord's faithful servants be regularly afflicted with discouragement, doubts, dryness, and bouts of sadness and anxiety? Why doesn't God prevent or remove pain and affliction?

Bad things happening to good people raises the problem of evil—the toughest philosophical and theological problem of all. The classic consideration of it in Scripture is the Book of Job. For no particularly good reason, God permits the devil to strike his faithful servant with terrible afflictions. When Job demands an explanation, God doesn't provide one. Instead he reminds Job that he is a mere creature, and that God is God. The afflictions were a test, and Job passed the test by remaining faithful. Ignatius doesn't tackle the philosophical problem of evil like the Book of Job does, but he addresses a subset of it. Why does God permit desolation?

Rule 9. The principal reasons why we suffer from desolation are three:

The first is because *we have been tepid and slothful or negligent* in our exercises of piety, and so through our own fault spiritual consolation has been taken away from us.

The second reason is because *God wishes to try us,* to see how much we are worth, and how much we will advance in His service and praise when left without the generous reward of consolations and signal favors.

The third reason is because *God wishes to give us a true knowledge and understanding of ourselves,* so that we may have an intimate perception of the fact that it is not within our power to acquire and attain great devotion, intense love, tears, or any other spiritual consolation; but that all this is the gift and grace of God our Lord. God does not wish us to build on the property of another, to rise up in spirit in a certain pride and vainglory and attribute to ourselves the devotion and other effects of spiritual consolation. (Emphasis added.)

The first reason is the one you'll probably think of first—desolation is somehow *my* fault; I've given in to a selfish desire, indulged a weakness, grown weak and tepid in prayer. God permits the desolation so we can become more diligent. The remedy is the advice of the sixth rule: "We can insist more upon prayer, upon meditation, and on much examination of ourselves." There's a sense in which desolation for this reason is inevitable and even desirable. We are flawed creatures; we are going to lose the emotional satisfaction of sensing God's presence from time to time. We will make mistakes. The desolation that comes will cause us to pray more, to seek God more diligently. To be prodded this way is a good thing.

The second reason for desolation is more complex. God permits desolation to try us, "to see how much we are worth." Ignatius's metaphor comes from the metallurgy of his time. Impurities were removed from gold by fire—quite literally, the trial by fire proved how much the gold was worth. This reason touches on one of the basic (and mysterious) aspects of God's creation. God does not compel us to love him. He created human beings as free creatures with the power to choose him or reject him. Our love of God is "for better or for worse." He cherishes our love when it comes from our free choice when loving isn't easy.

C. S. Lewis made this point well in *The Screwtape Letters*, a work of theological satire consisting of letters written by a senior demon named Screwtape to an apprentice explaining the ways of God (the Enemy). God will not override human will, Screwtape explains. "He cannot ravish. He can only woo." He continues:

> He wants them to learn to walk and must therefore take away His hand; and if only the will to walk is really there He is pleased even with their stumbles. Do not be deceived, Wormwood. Our cause is never more in danger than when a human, no longer desiring, but still intending to do our Enemy's will, looks round upon a universe from which every trace of Him seems to have vanished, and asks why he has been forsaken, and still obeys.

Our freedom is important to God. As the saying goes, the true test of someone's character is what they do when no one is looking.

The third reason why God permits desolation is "to give us a true knowledge and understanding of ourselves." God is the everlasting and ever-generous giver of gifts. He wants us to have an intimate and personal understanding of the fact that all blessings come from him and we can do nothing on our own. Regular experiences of desolation accomplish this. One day we are swimming along wonderfully in the great stream of grace and consolation, sure that all is well and is getting better. The next day the river has dried up and we are stuck with our same old disappointing selves. We reach out to God and beg for grace. Our sense of helplessness and need brings us back to consolation.

Ignatius valued humility as the greatest of virtues. Recall the Two Standards meditation: the enemy wants to lead us to monstrous pride and the good spirit wants to lead us to humility. In Ignatius's way of thinking, nothing is more dangerous than the notion that the world revolves around us. We want to be admired for the things we've achieved. We feel entitled to evaluate the shortcomings and mistakes of less impressive people. Ignatius thought that religious people were especially prone to a nasty form of this pride. People known for their rigorous prayer and great holiness often become closed and judgmental, hard on others and satisfied with themselves. His letters are full of warnings along these lines.

Regular bouts of desolation are a great antidote to spiritual pride. They bring us to the state of humble dependence on God that is true wisdom.

ACHIEVE SPIRITUAL BALANCE

Up to this point, Ignatius has been talking about coping with desolation while we are in the middle of experiencing desolation. The next two rules shift the focus to consolation.

Rule 10. When one enjoys consolation, let him consider how he will conduct himself during the time of ensuing desolation, and store up a supply of strength as defense against that day.

Rule 11. He who enjoys consolation should take care to humble himself and lower himself as much as possible. Let him recall how little he is able to do in time of desolation, when he is left without such grace or consolation. On the other hand, one who suffers desolation should remember that by making use of the sufficient grace offered him, he can do much to withstand all his enemies. Let him find his strength in his Creator and Lord.

Rule 10 is sometimes thought to mean that Ignatius is spoiling the party: "Don't get too caught up in consolation. Remember that desolation is coming." It actually means something close to the opposite. While we're feeling close to God, we're to make plans for what we'll do when he seems absent. We're to enjoy consolation to the utmost so what we have a store of grace to draw on when the rainy days come.

Ignatius says *consider* what you'll do when desolation comes. *Think about it.* In desolation, our thinking is muddled. We're not likely to spontaneously think of all the good advice that Ignatius has been offering in these rules—pray more, be patient, don't make any changes, and the rest. The time to think about these things is when we are enjoying consolation. Then we can decide that these are the things we'll do when desolation comes. In other words, our response to desolation should be consciously chosen.

Rule 11 is about achieving spiritual balance. It's something of a summation of all his advice up to this point. It suggests the proper way to respond to both consolation and desolation. Since consolation and desolation are contrary to each other, the responses to these states are contrary. The ideal is *balance.* It portrays the ideal discerning person—someone who is able to maintain spiritual equanimity and poise amid the alternating affective experiences of consolation and desolation.

The right response to consolation is *humility*: "He who enjoys consolation should take care to humble himself and lower himself as much as possible." The danger that comes with consolation is pride and the skewed perspective and faulty judgment that go along with pride. All is well; all is *wonderful*; there's nothing I can't do (with God's help, of course). A fine example is the apostle Peter. Even though he was one of Jesus's intimate friends, his boastfulness and inordinate self-confidence led him to a tragic failure. Humility is the goal; the ever-practical Ignatius suggests the ideal way to achieve it: *"Let him recall how little he is able to do in time of desolation."* You might be on top of the world now, but last week or last month the world was on top of you. You felt helpless and alone. You were begging the Lord for relief. Remember that you are just as dependent on God now, even though your confidence is boundless.

Desolation calls for the opposite response; instead of humility we're to cultivate confidence. *"One who suffers desolation should remember that by making use of the sufficient grace offered him, he can do much to withstand all his enemies."* Ignatius presumes that this isn't a new idea to the person in desolation. The person has surely felt confidence in God's grace previously, when he or she was experiencing consolation. Now's the time to remember this. No matter how helpless you feel, no matter how weak and confused, God's grace is sufficient to withstand any trial.

These responses involve a conscious decision to think a certain way. They won't well up spontaneously; the person in consolation isn't inclined to feel humble, and the person in desolation won't feel confident. We have to consciously bring these ideas to mind and follow through on them. Ignatian discernment largely involves the affective dimension of our personalities, but the practical mechanics of it involve judgment, choice, and interpretation. We need to experience our emotions fully, but we also need to stand apart from them. Underlying this rule—all the rules, for that matter—is Ignatius's vision of the spiritual life as something actively and consciously experienced. Spiritual persons aren't supposed to passively bob along waves of alternating consolation and desolation, like a boat in a storm. We're to be constantly aware of our spiritual experience. We're to be thoughtful and choose to think and behave in certain ways.

In Ignatian thinking, the right way to think and act is frequently to do the opposite of what you're feeling. In Ignatian circles this is called *agere contra,* Latin for "act against." It's an important principle of discernment. When considering possible choices, we will sometimes feel a great aversion to some options on the table. The question for discernment is "why?" Are there solid reasons for it, or do you resist because of a disordered attachment. If so, you might consider deliberately applying *agere contra* to it—act against it, and move past it.

THE ENEMY IS ESSENTIALLY WEAK

Ignatius shifts his teaching style in the last three rules for discernment. Up till now he has stated his point simply and tersely in a plain, unadorned style. Now he employs images and analogies to develop his ideas, using metaphors from the culture of his time. He talks about three things we need to know about the enemy: the evil spirit is essentially weak, it seeks to cloud its lies in secrecy, and it has a keen sense of our weak points.

Two of the metaphors Ignatius uses involve what we recognize today as sexual stereotypes. For the evil spirit's weakness, he describes a man facing down a shrewish woman. For secrecy, he uses the figure of a devious seducer telling women not to say anything about his evil suggestions. These metaphors worked in the sixteenth century, but today they don't work so well.

In Ignatius's defense (and in defense of the entire sixteenth century and all other centuries) it's generally an unsound practice to judge the past by the standards of the present. Every age operates with its own set of cultural assumptions and social norms that later ages find repugnant. No doubt this is true of our age as well. Five hundred years from now, people will be shocked at ideas and customs that seem obviously sound to us. We must try to understand past ages in their own terms, judging sparingly. Ignatius employed images familiar to readers in the sixteenth century; he grabbed the stereotypes off the cultural shelf, so to speak. He was not making points about the nature of women or men. It's enough to know that *some* people nag and badger others and that *some* lovers lie and betray to keep their seductions secret. Both men and women do these things—they did in Ignatius's time and they do in ours.

> **Rule 12.** The enemy conducts himself as a woman. He is a weakling before a show of strength, and a tyrant if he has his will. It is characteristic of a woman in a quarrel with a man to lose courage and to take flight if the man shows that he is determined and fearless. However, if the man loses courage and begins to flee, the anger, vindictiveness, and rage of the woman surge up and know no bounds. In the same way, the enemy becomes weak, loses courage, and turns to flight with his seductions as soon as one leading a spiritual life faces his temptations boldly, and does exactly the opposite of what he suggests. However, if one begins to be afraid and to lose courage in temptations, no wild animal on earth can be more fierce than the enemy of our human nature. He will carry out his perverse intentions with consummate malice.

The message of Rule 12 is that the enemy is essentially weak. When confronted firmly, the evil spirit backs down. It doesn't have the power to overcome a determined rebuff.

You might say, that's obvious. Of course the Lord is stronger than the devil. This is a point Ignatius has made often. Why repeat it here? The reason is that the rules for discernment are practical guides, not theological propositions, to be used in the heat of real-life spiritual turmoil. It's often the case that the enemy's essential weakness is not at all obvious when we're dealing with temptations, especially in times of desolation. *We* are the ones who feel weak and helpless. The enemy's temptations look unbearably powerful. *You'll never be able to resist this. It's only a matter of time. You've given in to this temptation many times before.* This is the time to be reminded that the enemy isn't as strong as he looks. We can vanquish the tempter by doing the exact opposite of what he suggests. This is another example of the Ignatian principle of *agere contra*—act against. Confront trouble. Don't wait for it to go away.

Rule 12 contains a couple of other practical insights into the psychology of spiritual struggle. Ignatius warns that a temptation can quickly get out of control if it's indulged. The first temptation is modest and reasonable. *Just this once. A little bit is OK. Just for today.* But giving in makes things worse. "He will carry out his perverse intentions with consummate malice." The evil one's strength increases; it becomes harder to resist the next temptation and soon we find ourselves in serious trouble. It follows that the best time to push back against the enemy is at the very beginning. Don't give into the first temptation. Don't wait to respond. Do the opposite of what the tempter suggests, and do it right away.

RESIST THE URGE TO KEEP THINGS TO YOURSELF

The baleful figure in Rule 13 is a devious, conniving man.

Rule 13. Our enemy may also be compared in his manner of acting to a false lover. He seeks to remain hidden and does not want to be discovered. If such a lover speaks with evil intention to the daughter of a good father, or to the wife of a good husband, and seeks to seduce them, he wants his words and solicitations kept secret. He is greatly displeased if his evil suggestions and depraved intentions are revealed by the daughter to her father, or by the wife to her husband. Then he readily sees he will not succeed in what he has begun. In the same way, when the enemy of our human nature tempts a just soul with his wiles and seductions, he earnestly desires that they be received secretly and kept secret. But if one manifests them to a confessor, or to some other spiritual person who understands his deceits and malicious designs, the evil one is very much vexed. For he knows that he cannot succeed in his evil undertaking, once his evident deceits have been revealed.

The enemy isn't proposing anything real and true. He's trading in lies—counterfeits and forgeries, disordered affections instead of the real thing, illusions, fancies, dreams, all wrapped up in pretty stories. The whole fraudulent edifice could come crashing down at any moment if it's exposed to the light of truth, so the enemy would like to keep things in the dark. He's in an essentially weak position as it is. His chances of success diminish even more if we call in reinforcements. So his message is *don't tell anyone about this.*

It's not hard to go along with this. Our spiritual struggles are personal; they usually involve urges and longings and temptations that we're not proud of. People don't know about them; most people *shouldn't* know about them. *This is an embarrassing problem. I'm ashamed of it. It's hard to talk about. No one would understand. If I talk about it I'll get into trouble.* Ignatius's analogy of the false lover actually fits pretty well. A woman who has been listening to a would-be seducer for a while might well hesitate to tell her husband or father about it. *It's better if I handle this on my own.* To the contrary, it's better to bring it into the light. That practically guarantees that the enemy's attack will fail.

It's important to talk about these struggles with the right person. Ignatius says it should be "a spiritual person who understands [the enemy's] deceits and malicious designs." This can be a confessor who knows the person well, or someone else, but the one essential qualification is skill in discernment. He or she must be "a spiritual person"—a person wise in spiritual matters, not a psychologist or a practical problem-solver. Sometimes psychological problems must be addressed, and problems almost always have to be solved, but this rule for discernment concerns spiritual matters. The person who hears the secrets must be someone who knows the spiritual realm.

Rule 13 is useful in another way. The urge to keep quiet about a thought or possibility or option for the future is a pretty good indicator that the idea comes from the evil spirit. Be suspicious when you don't want to talk about an idea that seems exciting to you.

KNOW YOUR WEAKNESSES

We've seen the enemy compared to an angry woman and a sly seducer. In Rule 14, the last of this set of rules, he's compared to a shrewd leader of a gang of brigands.

Rule 14. The conduct of our enemy may also be compared to the tactics of a leader intent upon seizing and plundering a position he desires. A commander and leader of an army will encamp, explore the fortifications and defenses of the stronghold, and attack at the weakest point. In the same way, the enemy of our human nature investigates from every side all our virtues, theological, cardinal, and moral. Where he finds the defenses of eternal salvation weakest and most deficient, there he attacks and tries to take us by storm.

Here the enemy is compared to an astute leader of fighting men. This is a more formidable guise than the angry woman and the sly seducer of the previous two rules, and the situation seems more ominous. A smart enemy is examining you carefully, looking for weaknesses. But Ignatius makes no suggestion that an attack is actually going to succeed. These last three rules assure us that the evil one's assault will fail. He will retreat if we resist him at the beginning (Rule 12). His edifice of lies will crumble if we bring it into the light (Rule 13). Rule 14 takes it a step further. By making adequate preparations, we can defeat the enemy *before* he attacks.

The message of Rule 14 is that each of us will face spiritual attacks designed for us personally. The rules for discernment have shown us the large patterns of the enemy's strategy—urging us to make impulsive changes, telling us that desolation will never end, that it is our fault, that God has abandoned us, that we can't tell anyone about this, and all the rest. The enemy attacks everyone in these ways, but he also attacks each individual at the point of their greatest vulnerability. "There he attacks and tries to take us by storm." The remedy is to know where our weaknesses are and build adequate defenses.

These fourteen rules show us how to handle desolation. But there's more to discernment. Consolation isn't always what it seems. That's the problem Ignatius explores in his second set of rules for discernment.

9

How Do I Know This Is from God?

Ignatius's first bit of news is that we are desolation's clients. The spirits of alienation and anxiety will come calling regularly, and it's important that we learn to ignore their sales pitches and cut their visits short. Ignatius's second bit of news has to do with consolation. Consolation is almost always ambiguous and frequently treacherous, he tells us. Those feelings of peace, well-being, and energetic optimism aren't necessarily signs of God's presence and blessing. They can be tools of the evil one seeking to deflect us from the path that leads to true joy.

This is an unwelcome fact, but hardly a surprising one. If consolation was always a foolproof sign of God's leading, you wouldn't be reading this book. There wouldn't be much need for discernment. Just do what you feel good about.

Here's the truth of the matter as Ignatius puts it in the first of eight rules for "a more accurate discernment of spirits."

Rule 1. It is characteristic of God and His Angels, when they act upon the soul, to give true happiness and spiritual joy, and to banish all the sadness and disturbances which are caused by the enemy.

It is characteristic of the evil one to fight against such happiness and consolation by proposing fallacious reasonings, subtleties, and continual deceptions.

This is why we need discernment. With one partial exception (which we'll discuss in a minute), no feeling, leading, insight, or inner conviction is unquestionably a sign of God's presence. The devil can mimic consolation. Every movement of our spirits needs to be examined, weighed, pondered, and interpreted to determine whether it's from God or from "the enemy of our human nature," to use one of Ignatius's favorite terms for the spiritual entities who would drag us down. It's not a good idea to act simply because you have a strong conviction that "the Lord wants me to do this." That's naive. Our enemy is too shrewd, and our tendency to find reasons to do what we want to do is too strong, for this to be a sound principle for the spiritual life.

The enemy sows trouble and confusion with "fallacious reasonings, subtleties, and continual deceptions," according to Ignatius. *Fallacious reasonings* (or "apparent reasons" in another translation) refers to our inclination to deceive ourselves. We have a strong penchant for deciding what we want to do and then finding any number of reasons for doing it. We think that a decision is the result of careful reasoning when it's really driven by disordered attachments.

Ignatius speaks of the enemy's use of *subtleties*. This is the thicket of problems, doubts, and complexities that emerge when we set out on a course of action that we think is the right one. We discover reasons not to do the right thing. A good plan suddenly looks too difficult to implement. These problems are subtle. Often they're not entirely without foundation.

The enemy employs "*continual* deceptions," or "*persistent* fallacies" as another translation has it. Flawed ideas and unsupported doubts stick around after we think we have banished them.

We find ourselves battling the same problems over and over again. Recall Ignatius's image of the enemy as the commander of a gang of brigands coolly surveying a victim's defenses, looking for weak spots. We can shore up the weak defenses, but the weaknesses never go away completely.

Fortunately, it's always possible to detect the enemy's deceptions. God and his angels give "*true* happiness and spiritual joy." The evil one may be resourceful and shrewd, but he can't produce authentic consolation. He can only imitate it, manufacture a good-looking forgery, and tell a pretty story. There's always a difference between genuine consolation and the evil one's version. Discernment is about telling the difference between the two.

WHEN YOU *KNOW* IT'S FROM GOD

There's a partial exception to the axiom that every movement of consolation must be tested and discerned. This is what Ignatius calls "consolation without previous cause." This is the perception of divine grace that comes without explanation and usually without warning—"out of the blue" as we say. Sometimes, literally out of the blue, a feeling of deep peace, or a palpable sense that God is speaking to you personally, seems to come suddenly from the heavens. When you have this kind of consolation you can be sure it's from God.

Here's what Ignatius says about it:

> **Rule 2**. God alone can give consolation to the soul without any previous cause. It belongs solely to the Creator to come into a soul, to leave it, to act upon it, to draw it wholly to the love of His Divine Majesty. I said without previous cause, that is, without any preceding

perception or knowledge of any subject by which a soul might be led to such a consolation through its own acts of intellect and will.

Ignatius is talking about consolation that comes to us without the help of memories, ideas, images, and sensory impressions. A feeling of deep connection to God that comes as you watch a beautiful sunset is not consolation without previous cause. Neither is a feeling of profound peace that you experience at Mass, or tears of joy that well up while you listen to Mozart's *Requiem*. These consolations have a cause—natural beauty, worship, music—and they need further examination and interpretation before you can conclude that they are true spiritual consolations.

At first, it seems rather hard to imagine consolation without previous cause. After all, we are sensory creatures, dependent on vision, hearing, touch, taste, and smell for virtually everything we experience. Yet many people have had experiences of spiritual joy and peace and blessing that come unexpectedly and seem to be directly from God. Often our tendency is to dismiss such things, but Ignatius says we can simply enjoy them. Only God can access our souls directly. The evil one cannot produce a consolation without cause. It's a special blessing from God; there's no need to apply the other tools of discernment to judge whether it's authentic.

Experts in Ignatian spirituality tend to emphasize the rarity of these experiences. They certainly aren't the norm, but perhaps they happen more frequently than you might suspect. You're in the midst of an extended "spiritual drought." God seems far away; prayer is difficult. Or you are struggling with difficult life circumstances—illness, family problems, financial difficulties. All the circumstances would point toward desolation, yet in the midst of these troubles you feel a profound peace and a conviction that all will be well. This is not an uncommon experience. Might this be consolation without previous cause?

It's another matter to make a decision on the basis of a revelation that you think comes directly from God. This does happen; the best-known example is Saul of Tarsus, the scourge of Christians, stricken by a vision from Christ that changed his life completely. Such divine interventions are very rare. God normally leads us and speaks to us through more ordinary means. Ignatius warns about the danger of making decisions in the aftermath of a consolation without cause in another rule of discernment:

> **Rule 8.** When consolation is without previous cause, as was said, there can be no deception in it, since it can proceed from God our Lord only. But a spiritual person who has received such a consolation *must consider it very attentively, and must cautiously distinguish the actual time of the consolation from the period which follows it.* At such a time the soul is still fervent and favored with the grace and aftereffects of the consolation which has passed. In this second period the soul frequently forms various resolutions and plans which are not granted directly by God our Lord. They may come from our own reasoning on the relations of our concepts and on the consequences of our judgments, or they may come from the good or evil spirit. Hence, they must be carefully examined before they are given full approval and put into execution. (Emphasis added.)

The "afterglow" of a spiritual experience turns out to be a dangerous time. The good spirit can operate here, but so can the evil spirit. We can make impulsive, ill-considered decisions in the aftermath of a deep experience of God, convinced that "the

Lord told me to do this." It turns out that consolation without previous cause is only a partial exception to the rule that every spiritual experience needs to be examined and discerned. We can be sure that the consolation itself is from God, but once we consider doing something different on the basis of such a consolation, the other tools of discernment come into play.

THE REAL QUESTION IN DISCERNMENT

In any case, consolations without cause are not the norm. God doesn't often operate directly on our souls. Usually consolations have a cause; they come through our senses and our minds, responding to the circumstances of our lives. The normal way to encounter God is through our own natural faculties.

This isn't a novel idea, yet there's something in us that resists it. We sometimes think that the *real* spiritual experiences are the "supernatural" ones—the vision, the dramatic conversion, the striking insight that comes out of the blue, the glorious leading that comes unexpectedly in prayer. Other experiences of God aren't as clear and vivid, so we find ourselves asking, "Is this experience from God or is it just my own imagination?" In the Ignatian perspective, they are *almost always* from your imagination (and your senses and your intellect). This is the way we normally encounter God—through what we see and hear, and what we think and imagine. It's also the way we encounter the evil one. So the real question for discernment is, "Is God working in me through this consolation, or is it from the evil spirit?" Here's how Ignatius puts it:

> **Rule 3.** If a cause precedes, both the good angel and the evil spirit can give consolation to a soul, but for a quite different purpose. The good angel consoles for the

progress of the soul, that it may advance and rise to what is more perfect. The evil spirit consoles for purposes that are the contrary, and that afterwards he might draw the soul to his own perverse intentions and wickedness.

Desolation, the subject of Ignatius's first set of rules, is pretty clear-cut. Sadness, anxiety, self-loathing, and the rest are always from the evil spirit. God may permit desolation, but he never causes it. It's sometimes quite difficult to deal with desolation, but we don't have to worry about determining whether it's from God or the enemy. On the other hand, consolation is ambiguous. It can come either from the Holy Spirit or the evil spirit. It can mean very different things.

This rule, like all the other rules for discernment, is based on Ignatius's personal experience. He knew about false consolation firsthand. In his autobiography he describes two times of consolation that appeared to be good but turned out to be false. Both times, a profound consolation came repeatedly at night. He stayed awake a long time, enjoying the experience, until he realized that the lost sleep was making him weary and unable to do his work well. This experience illustrates something important about discerning consolations. True consolation and false consolation both feel genuine. We can't tell the difference by identifying some quality of the consolation itself. We discern consolation by judging something external to it—usually its effects. The evil spirit consoles so that "*afterwards* he might draw the soul to his own perverse intentions and wickedness."

ANGEL OF LIGHT

It's been established that consolation needs to be examined carefully; we can't just assume that it's from God. The rest of the rules have to do with the practicalities of this discernment. The first idea to establish firmly in our minds is that the evil one will be disguised. "Satan disguises himself as an angel of light," says St. Paul in a passage warning about false apostles (see 2 Cor 11:14). Ignatius picks up Paul's language:

> **Rule 4.** It is a mark of the evil spirit to assume the appearance of an angel of light. He begins by suggesting thoughts that are suited to a devout soul, and ends by suggesting his own. For example, *he will suggest holy and pious thoughts* that are wholly in conformity with the sanctity of the soul. Afterwards, he will endeavor little by little to end by drawing the soul into his hidden snares and evil designs. (Emphasis added.)

The evil spirit can be the source of our "holy and pious thoughts." This is perhaps the most troubling of Ignatius's observations about the spiritual life. Desires to do great deeds for God don't protect us from serious mistakes. Yearnings to pray more and to act more generously don't inoculate us from trouble. In fact, these very impulses might lead us astray. They may have been planted in us by our enemy to deflect us from the true path. This shouldn't be a surprise. Look around: Wise people become critical of those who don't see things their way. Good leaders become rigid and controlling. Movements for reform lurch into excess, and become forces for division. Who has not had the experience of embarking on a new path of spiritual renewal only to be bitterly disappointed when it doesn't work out the way she or he had hoped?

Determining what we really want is difficult. It's hard enough to see how money, power, prestige, sex, and other well-known dangers can take us to bad places. But we must also contend with the fact that our yearning for holiness, for community, for service to others can take us off track too. To discern well, we need a good measure of humility and caution, and a healthy skepticism about our own motives.

WHAT'S THE OUTCOME?

Ignatius says that the problems come "afterwards." First come the holy and pious thoughts. We entertain them and act on them, and the deception comes "little by little." There's a *process* of deception. Ignatius's next rule describes it.

> **Rule 5.** We must carefully observe the whole course of our thoughts. If the beginning and middle and end of the course of thoughts are wholly good and directed to what is entirely right, it is a sign that they are from the good angel. But the course of thoughts suggested to us may terminate in something evil, or distracting, or less good than the soul had formerly proposed to do. Again, it may end in what weakens the soul, or disquiets it; or by destroying the peace, tranquility, and quiet which it had before, it may cause disturbance to the soul. These things are a clear sign that the thoughts are proceeding from the evil spirit, the enemy of our progress and eternal salvation.

This rule draws our attention to how it all turns out. We can tell whether the consolation was from God or from the enemy by looking at the outcome of the process.

It might result in something *evil*, says Ignatius. This might not happen very often, but scandals and moral evil involving Christians are hardly unheard of. More often, the outcome can be *something bad*, as another translation of the rule puts it. A marriage can be damaged when one partner spends too much time on apostolic projects outside the home. A parish can be divided when the pastor pushes a pet project too hard. A person can grow bitter when ideas that they think come straight from God are rejected.

Many bad consequences of false consolations are more subtle, falling into the category of things that *don't* happen. They are *distracting* or *less good*, as Ignatius puts it. We get distracted from responsibilities and projects and people because we're very busy now with the exciting new venture. Friends, children, and spouses are neglected. Important tasks are left undone. Ignatius recounts how he was distracted from his studies by "new understandings of spiritual things and new delights." The consolations would come every time he sat down at his desk to study, and he found it quite difficult to get free of the distractions. We can also identify a false consolation when the consequences are *less good* than what was happening previously. A person might withdraw from a successful volunteer job "to spend more time with the Lord." A new program that begins with passion ends in tears, draining resources from other programs in the process.

Another sign of false consolation is disturbance and lack of peace. We're noisy and agitated. The soul's tranquility and quiet vanish. Ignatius develops this point further in another rule.

This rule (and all the others for that matter) implies that we are able to maintain a continuing awareness of the spiritual movements of our inner life. We're to keep track of "the whole course of our thoughts"—beginning, middle, and end. False consolation is a process, and discernment is too. We don't "do" discernment at special times.

HOW DID THIS HAPPEN?

The pious project hasn't turned out well. You're frustrated and depressed. People are angry with you. You're in a worse place now than you were when you started. What do you do now? One answer is to cut your losses. *"That's yesterday's news." "I apologize; let's move on now."* Not so fast, Ignatius says. We should look back and understand how the disaster happened.

> **Rule 6.** When the enemy of our human nature has been detected and recognized by the trail of evil marking his course and by the wicked end to which he leads us, it will be profitable for one who has been tempted to review immediately the whole course of the temptation. Let him consider the series of good thoughts, how they arose, how the evil one gradually attempted to make him step down from the state of spiritual delight and joy in which he was, till finally he drew him to his wicked designs. The purpose of this review is that once such an experience has been understood and carefully observed, we may guard ourselves for the future against the customary deceits of the enemy.

This rule focuses on the middle part of the process. We can identify the consolation as a false one by looking at its outcome. Now we look back at how the process unfolded in order to understand how things went wrong.

The purpose of this review, says Ignatius, is *"to guard ourselves for the future against the customary deceits of the enemy."* This means that the enemy's false consolation exploited weaknesses, habits, and impulses that are uniquely yours. Maybe you have a tendency to ignore advice from others. Or you're excitable and inclined to excess. Maybe your desire to "make a difference" makes you receptive to grandiose ill-conceived schemes. Or perhaps you are profoundly dissatisfied with your life and are drawn to anything that promises to make things better. Ignatius wants us to engage in this review, painful as it may be, because we will certainly be attacked again in the same way. If we know our weaknesses, we'll be better able to avoid trouble the next time.

Ignatius's emphasis here is on *awareness* of our weaknesses. He doesn't speak of fixing them. It would certainly be ideal if we corrected the problems, but his assumption seems to be that we will continue to be impulsive, grandiose, proudly independent, mildly depressed, or whatever our weaknesses may be. Ignatius's aim here is to help us change the way we relate to our flaws, not to get rid of them.

It's interesting to note how this rule anticipates the practices of modern psychology. A widely-used therapeutic method today is Cognitive-Behavioral therapy, which attempts to overcome maladaptive behavior by making people aware of their destructive thought patterns. CB therapists don't try to "cure" a person's anger, or self-loathing, or depression. They teach people to notice how they are thinking when they get angry, or anxious, or depressed. Then they change their thinking instead of lashing out, or taking a drug, or isolating themselves.

DISCERNMENT AT THE BEGINNING

Is it possible to identify a false consolation at the beginning, when the bad idea first presents itself? We can discern the enemy's handiwork by evaluating the outcome and by examining the gradual step-by-step process by which an apparently attractive proposition goes wrong. But this is after-the-fact discernment. It would be much better to detect trouble before it gets started. Ignatius thinks so too:

> **Rule 7.** In souls that are progressing to greater perfection, the action of the good angel is delicate, gentle, delightful. It may be compared to a drop of water penetrating a sponge.

The action of the evil spirit upon such souls is violent, noisy, and disturbing. It may be compared to a drop of water falling upon a stone.

In souls that are going from bad to worse, the action of the spirits mentioned above is just the reverse. The reason for this is to be sought in the opposition or similarity of these souls to the different kinds of spirits. When the disposition is contrary to that of the spirits, they enter with noise and commotion that are easily perceived. When the disposition is similar to that of the spirits, they enter silently, as one coming into his own house when the doors are open.

This rule is about identifying spiritual dissonance. We're not looking at results—angry friends and family, neglected responsibilities, problems piling up, a dark mood descending. This is pure discernment of spirits. Does the new spiritual movement fit our spiritual disposition or does it strike a dissonant note, like a jarring note in a pleasing melody? If our spiritual condition is basically healthy, God's action will be gentle and delightful, like "a drop of water penetrating a sponge." The action of the enemy will be noisy and disturbing, like "a drop of water falling upon a stone."

This kind of discernment requires great spiritual sensitivity. Ignatius's examples suggest as much: a drop of water falling on a stone doesn't make much noise, and water soaking into a sponge doesn't attract much attention. A false consolation is dangerous precisely because it's a consolation. The proposition seems attractive and plausible. It looks good. We're excited and inspired by it. But false consolation isn't the real thing. There's always something fallacious and unsound about the evil spirit's version of consolation. The problems always show up over time, but the falseness is there from the beginning, and with practice we can learn to detect it. We're looking for subtle signs: a nagging doubt, a feeling that something isn't right, a foreshadowing of spiritual trouble.

Ignatius's image of water falling on a rock is merely suggestive; it's not a practical description of these subtle signs. A couple of much-admired spiritual writers offer more concrete examples of the impulses that indicate that a consolation might be a false one.

The first is the French Jesuit Maurice Giuliani, who was an important leader of the renewal of Ignatian spirituality in the years following the Second Vatican Council. Giuliani thought that the appropriate spiritual response to a new undertaking that comes from God is usually one of confusion and humility. *Why me? I can't do this. Lord, I am not worthy.* This was the reaction of Moses, Isaiah, and Mary. It was the reaction of Jesus himself at Gethsemane. The next step is surrender to God, followed by resolute and loving dedication to the task. The outcome is peace. The response is the opposite when a consolation comes from the evil one. The initial response is excessive confidence and excitement. Humility is nowhere to be found. The next step is frustration when obstacles present themselves, followed by discouragement and hopelessness. In the end the project is abandoned and the person is in a worse place than before. Giuliani suggests that in discerning false consolation, we should look for humility at the beginning.

Another helpful insight about bad beginnings comes from C. S. Lewis. He said that the choice that eventually leads to moral evil is often motivated by a desire to join "the inner ring"— the in-group, the elite, the witty, attractive person you admire so much. Someone in the inner ring invites you to do something that seems not quite right. You will be drawn in, says Lewis, "not by desire for gain or ease, but simply because at that moment, when the cup was so near your lips, you cannot bear to be thrust back again into the cold outer world. It would be so terrible to see the other man's face—that genial, confidential, delightfully sophisticated face—turn suddenly cold and contemptuous, to know that you had been tried for the Inner Ring and rejected." Many unsound decisions are made like this. We want to join the club. We want to ally ourselves with prestigious institutions and smart people who think we are smart too. We don't want to disappoint people we admire. It's easier to say yes than to say no.

It's difficult to do this kind of sensitive discernment successfully. We have to know ourselves very well to sort out the mixed motives that go into every choice. Few of us measure up. Ignatius assumes that you're not trying to do this alone. He repeatedly stresses the importance of having a spiritual director or a trusted friend or two who can help you with discernment.

A DISCERNING STATE OF MIND

Ignatius's twenty-two rules for discernment are not "rules" in the scientific or mathematical sense—a universally valid "law of nature" that describes how things always work. The spiritual life is inherently ambiguous to our human minds. Ignatius's observations about it are generalizations; they are rules in the sense of "as a general rule. . . ." They are best practices for playing offense and defense in a game. The rules of the first set are about defense—how to keep desolation in check so it does no lasting harm. The rules of the second set are about offense—how to get closer to our goal of finding what we really want by distinguishing the voice of the good spirit from the voice of the enemy.

The rules are often called a "toolkit" for discernment, like a carpenter's belt studded with pliers, drills, screwdrivers, hammers, and other tools for a remodeling job. But that too implies more lucidity and precision than spiritual discernment possesses in reality. The rules are more like the operating assumptions of someone with a discerning state of mind.

The discerning mind is especially valuable when it comes time to make a decision. That's what we turn to next.

10

Good and Bad Decisions

We certainly need help making decisions. Our thinking is skewed by a host of what psychologists call "cognitive biases." We think we have more control over people and events than we actually do. We prefer small immediate benefits to greater long-term benefits. When we think about the future, we give more weight to the most recent thing that happened (the stock is up ten percent this month!) than to more distant events (the stock is still down for the year). We'll see patterns in past events where none actually exist. We underestimate the time it will take to finish a job. We overestimate our ability to resist temptation and to show restraint. When good things happen, we think we're responsible. When things turn sour, it's not our fault. The biggest problem in decision making is "confirmation bias." Most of the time we have a good idea of what we want to do, and will systematically look for reasons to do it and ignore reasons not to. If you think that you're immune to cognitive biases, you have lots of company. Most people think they're smarter, more accurate, luckier, and more objective than everybody else. It almost seems that any decision that works out well does so by accident.

No doubt Ignatius became well acquainted with the haphazard nature of decision making during many years working with people who were trying to decide the direction for their lives. He devotes a considerable amount of attention to decision making in the *Spiritual Exercises*. Discernment and decision making are not synonymous in the Ignatian tradition. Discernment is a skill and an art, but it's also an attitude of reflective awareness that can guide us all the time. Decision making is a process. Discernment is a big part of it, but in the *Spiritual Exercises*, decision making is a topic unto itself.

DECISIONS HAVE LIMITS

Ignatius doesn't offer any kind of a guarantee about decisions. Decisions, even good and well-made decisions, are cloaked in uncertainty. Discernment doesn't give knowledge of the future. It doesn't say what other people are going to do in connection with your decision. It doesn't guarantee that the new project or new job or marriage will be a success. It doesn't even promise that the choice you make will happen at all. You might decide you should be married but never find someone whom you want to marry (and who wants to marry you). After thorough reflection and discernment you might decide to apply for that new job, but the job might go to someone else. Pope Francis was speaking from the Ignatian tradition when he said that "uncertainty is in every true discernment. The risk in seeking and finding God in all things is the willingness to explain too much, to say with human certainty and arrogance: 'God is here.'"

Ignatius's own life is an ironic commentary on his renown as an expert on decision making. Many of his decisions, including some very important ones, didn't turn out as he thought they would. After his conversion he went to the Holy Land, thinking that God wanted him to spend his life there; the

Church authorities in Jerusalem sent him back to Europe. He thought he should fast strenuously, punish his body, and practice other severe penances; this permanently damaged his health and caused great spiritual misery. Twice he refused the office of superior general after his brother Jesuits elected him; his confessor had to practically order him to change his mind. He thought the Jesuits should own very little property; in his lifetime they ended up running an international network of schools, becoming champion fundraisers and smart money managers in the process. He thought that God wanted him to be an itinerant teacher, preacher, and evangelist; he spent the last fourteen years of his life running the Jesuits from a small suite of offices in Rome.

Ignatius didn't think that making good decisions was the most important thing in the Christian life. For him, decisions were a means, not an end. They take us toward God or away from him. "Our one desire and choice should be what is more conducive to the end for which we are created," as he put it in the Principle and Foundation. In most circumstances we can be reasonably confident that a well-made decision is the right one. But a decision is one step; we don't know very much about the next step, and the step after that. And any decision you make is a decision just for you. It doesn't apply to anyone else.

When he was head of the Jesuits, Ignatius became alarmed when Pope Julius III said that he wanted to make another Jesuit a cardinal. Ignatius opposed this plan because the office of cardinal at that time brought with it wealth and a luxurious style of life. Jesuits were committed to poverty; the prospect of a Jesuit cardinal seriously undermined the way he thought Jesuits should live and what they should stand for. He lobbied hard to scuttle the pope's plans, writing, "If I did not act thus,

I would be quite certain that I would not give a good account of myself before God our Lord." However, others took a contrary view; they welcomed the idea of a Jesuit cardinal and they made their views known. Ignatius did not oppose this. He said that others were free to disagree with him, writing that "the same Spirit could inspire me to take one point of view for some reasons and inspire others to the contrary for other reasons."

Consider Ignatius's attitude in light of what we've learned about discernment. Ignatius thought he was right; he had prayed about his decision and thought it was the correct one for the good of the Jesuit order. But he was open to the possibility that the those opposing him could be right too. They both might be right. God could be moving people on both sides of the question to hold the views they had. God could be allowing this clash of views for some larger purpose. Ignatius recognized that there was much he didn't know—and could never know—about how events would unfold in God's plan.

Nevertheless, Ignatius thought that we can have confidence in our decisions. We can't know the future, but we can be reasonably sure that we can discern the best option available to us in our present circumstances. He proposes a methodology for making decisions (more about that in the next chapter), but more important than the process is the spiritual foundations of a good decision.

LOVE GOD FIRST

In the Ignatian perspective, the decision isn't the most important thing. It's the means, not the end. The biggest mistake we make when we come to make an important decision is confusing ends and means, Ignatius writes:

I must not subject and fit the end to the means, but the means to the end. Many first choose marriage, which is a means, and secondarily the service of God our Lord in marriage, though the service of God is the end. So also others first choose to have benefices, and afterwards to serve God in them. Such persons do not go directly to God, but want God to conform wholly to their inordinate attachments. Consequently, they make of the end a means, and of the means an end. As a result, what they ought to seek first, they seek last.

God is the end; the decision is a way to get there. Our end is to "praise, reverence, and serve God our Lord," as the Principle and Foundation says. The "things on the face of the earth"—jobs, people, money, knowledge, art, science, everything—are there to help us achieve this end.

Much of the time we have it backward. We make the decision first (employing wishful thinking, selective memory, cognitive biases, and disordered affections) and then ask God to bless it. I will be a lawyer, an entrepreneur, a teacher—and I'll serve God too. I'll get married—and pray that the marriage will be successful. I'll pray that the new job I'm taking will turn out well—after I've decided to take that new job. These prayers aren't in vain; God will bless you. But this isn't the best approach to decisions. God comes first; then comes the decision.

Decisions carry us along on our journey to God. Decisions lead to more decisions. The outcome is out of our control. If Plan A doesn't work out, there's always Plan B—and Plans C, D, E, and F. Plenty of Ignatius's Plan As failed, but he marched along steadily, seeking always to love God and to bring the good news of salvation to others. So it is with us. We're on a path to God, and it's not necessarily a linear path. It can be a meandering one, with cul-de-sacs and dead ends, tangents and digressions. It's more like a spiral—a process of reflection, choice, further reflection, more choice—that carries us deeper into a life lived more and more for God.

Seeking God above all else is the first requirement for making a good decision. It's the one necessary thing. It's what Jesus meant in his words about the kingdom of God. "The kingdom of heaven is like treasure hidden in a field, which someone found and hid; then in his joy he goes and sells all that he has and buys that field. Again, the kingdom of heaven is like a merchant in search of fine pearls; on finding one pearl of great value, he went and sold all that he had and bought it" (Mt 13:44-46).

THE CALL OF THE KING

Seeking the kingdom of God above all other things is the theme of an exercise in the *Spiritual Exercises* called The Call of the King. Ignatius asks us to imagine an immensely powerful and terrifically charismatic earthly king inviting us to join him in his work:

> Consider the address this king makes to all his subjects, with the words: "It is my will to conquer all the lands of the infidel. Therefore, whoever wishes to join with me in this enterprise must be content with the same food, drink, clothing, etc., as mine. So, too, he must work with me by day, and watch with me by night, etc., that as he had a share in the toil with me, afterwards, he may share in the victory with me."

This exercise needs some cultural translation for an age that looks dubiously at imagery involving armies, kings, and great crusades. Europeans in the sixteenth century looked to great leaders to fulfill their dreams for a good and just world. They longed for a Good King (and a Good Pope) who would right all wrongs, bring justice to the realm, rule with wisdom, and vanquish enemies. Ignatius and his friends and followers felt this yearning viscerally, so an invitation to join the army of a great and good king packs a punch for them that's largely lost on us. But we too yearn for justice and righteousness. We long to see evil vanquished, the world at peace, a world where "the blind receive their sight, the lame walk, the lepers are cleansed, the deaf hear, the dead are raised, and the poor have good news brought to them" (Mt 11:5). If the king leaves you cold, imagine the invitation coming from someone who taps into your longing to be part of a great effort to do good. It might be a project to feed the hungry in your community, or to bring healing to people afflicted with disease. The leader is addressing you personally: "Come, join us in this." You'd probably respond positively in some way. Ignatius assumes as much. He says that the subjects of such a "generous and noble-minded king" will respond to this invitation with enthusiasm.

He then asks us to imagine that the king is Christ, inviting us to join him in the work of conquering the whole world for the kingdom of God. "Whoever wishes to join me in this enterprise must be willing to labor with me, that by following me in suffering, he may follow me in glory." How would you respond to *this* invitation? *Of course* you'd want to follow Christ. If you responded positively to the earthly leader's invitation, you'd be even more enthusiastic about following Christ.

The really interesting part of the Call of the King exercise is what Ignatius has to say about our response to Christ's call. We might respond in two different ways. The first is the "reasonable" response. This is what a normal, sensible Christian would do upon hearing an invitation to join Christ in his work. Of course you'd sign up. Who wouldn't? Ignatius writes, "All persons who have judgment and reason will offer themselves entirely for this work."

But you could go further—much further. In Ignatius's words, those who want to do more "will not only offer themselves entirely for the work, but will act against their sensuality and carnal and worldly love, and make offerings of greater value and of more importance." You can write a check to support the program to feed the hungry—or you could go all in. Feeding the hungry could become your calling in life. You could go to medical school and devote your career as a physician to eradicating disease in Africa. This is the kind of response that Ignatius is after—eagerness to "make offerings of greater value and of more importance."

This is the famous "*magis*" of Ignatian spirituality. "*Magis*" is a Latin word meaning *more*. It's been called the Jesuit "itch"—an ambition to reach greater heights, to conquer new frontiers, to maintain the highest standards. The word simply means *more*. "*Magis*" has more to do with the quality of our personal commitment to Christ than with long hours and a crowded schedule. God loves us without limit. We love him in return, but we're always looking for what *more* we can do to love him.

The Call of the King exercise highlights the essential requirement for making a good decision. Our first desire should be to respond to the call of Christ as fully and generously as we can. This is what we desire most deeply. This is what we really want.

The obstacle to fulfilling our deepest desires is our old friend disordered attachments. We don't know what we really want because it's buried under a pile of yearnings for money, success, luxury, sex, honor, power, and other things that crowd out most authentic desires. The first requirement for a sound decision is to love God first. The second requirement is to identify these disordered attachments and neutralize them.

THREE KINDS OF HUMILITY

Confronting disordered attachments is the theme of a meditation in the *Spiritual Exercises* called the Three Kinds of Humility. This is not an imaginative exercise like the Three Classes of People and the Two Standards, but is straight propositional material—three kinds of humility, described in the abstract, set forth for our consideration. The point of the exercise isn't to find fault. All three kinds of humility are worthy. In fact, at any one time, we might see all three kinds operating in ourselves.

The first kind of humility is to conform oneself to God's law:

> **The First Kind:** This is necessary for salvation. It consists in this, that as far as possible I so subject and humble myself as to obey the law of God our Lord and in all things, so that not even were I made lord of all creation, or to save my life here on earth, would I consent to violate a commandment, whether divine or human, that binds me under pain of mortal sin.

The first kind of humility is no small task; living a righteous life means beating back temptations and struggling to do the right thing. But it's the least we can do. A wholehearted decision to join yourself with Christ in his work needs more than the minimum.

The second kind of humility ups the ante:

The Second Kind: This is more perfect than the first. I possess it if my attitude of mind is such that I neither desire nor am I inclined to have riches rather than poverty, to seek honor rather than dishonor, to desire a long life rather than a short life, provided only in either alternative I would promote equally the service of God our Lord and the salvation of my soul.

This humility is the kind of freedom that Ignatius talked about in the Three Classes exercise. Ignatius repeats the words of the Principle and Foundation: we don't want to seek "riches rather than poverty, to seek honor rather than dishonor, to desire a long life rather than a short one." This is Ignatian "indifference"—the freedom from disordered attachments that allows us to discern what we really want.

Finally, there's the third kind of humility:

The Third Kind: This is the most perfect kind of humility. It consists in this. If we suppose the first and second kind attained, then whenever the praise and glory of the Divine Majesty would be equally served, in order to imitate and be in reality more like Christ our Lord, I desire and choose poverty with Christ poor, rather than riches; insults with Christ loaded with them, rather than honors; I desire to be accounted as worthless and a fool for Christ, rather than to be esteemed as wise and prudent in this world. So Christ was treated before me.

Those aspiring to the third kind of humility are not only detached from the things most people want; they positively desire the opposite. They *want* poverty, dishonor, and humiliation. They're able to say, "I desire to be accounted as worthless and a fool for Christ, rather than be esteemed as wise and prudent in this world."

It's difficult to grasp what the third kind of humility means. Over the centuries many have taken it to mean that we should choose the most painful and difficult path out of love for Christ. It's also hard to imagine someone actually living day-to-day with the mindset of a person with the third kind of humility. To do your work well, you have to want it to succeed, not fail. You want people's respect, not their insults.

Some cultural translation helps. Ignatius wrote this exercise while he was a student at the University of Paris, the best university in Europe. He lived among ambitious young men preparing for careers in a society that especially valued status and honor. The coin of the realm in their world was what other people thought of you, especially what powerful bishops, aristocrats, and potential benefactors thought of you. Therefore, Ignatius invites these men to consider what it would mean to turn their backs on the thing that they valued most highly. Could they embrace dishonor and humiliation, to say, "I desire to be accounted as worthless and a fool for Christ, rather than be esteemed as wise and prudent in this world."

The point of the exercise is to get us to identify those things we can't do without. It asks, "What are your nonnegotiables?" For sixteenth-century aristocrats it was being held in high esteem by others. Today it probably has more to do with money, success, and power. What are *your* nonnegotiables? What preconceived ideas do you have about how you will follow Christ? Perhaps you need to be a leader, giving direction and setting the pace; perhaps you see yourself as a follower, serving humbly on a team. Maybe you need to accomplish something noteworthy. Maybe financial security comes first. Perhaps your heart is set on a certain style of service—a desk job, hands-on work, the life of the mind. The exercise asks you to imagine doing without those cherished ideas. It doesn't mean that the best way to serve God is the most unpleasant, difficult, and personally disagreeable way. It doesn't mean that you must go against the grain of your personality to be a true disciple. In fact, it means something like the opposite: God wants our life with him to fulfill our deepest desires for ourselves. He will lead us to the life we're suited for, but to get there we need to put aside *our* cherished ideas of what we're suited for.

DISCERNMENT AND DECISIONS

It's important to understand that Ignatius's exercises are exercises. They are intended to get us to think; they don't describe an ideal of perfect detachment and freedom that we will attain one day if we try hard enough. We will never be completely free of our disordered attachments. We are human beings with clouded minds and divided hearts. As long as we live there will be conflict between what we most deeply desire and our confused and conflicted ideas of what will make us happy. What we *can* do is minimize the influence of our disordered attachments on our decisions.

Skill in discernment of spirits is the final requirement for making a good decision. Ignatius's genius was to see that the very conflict in our divided hearts provides the insight we need to find what we really want. The contest between the evil spirit and the Holy Spirit produces feelings of consolation and desolation. This is the raw material for discernment.

We need to see the decision as part of the "big picture." It's a choice driven by the desire to love and follow Christ. To make it we need to become detached from our nonnegotiables, so we can say, with Paul, that "I regard everything as loss because of the surpassing value of knowing Christ Jesus my Lord" (Phil 3:8).

Finally, we need to be able to discern the spirits in an attitude of reflective awareness that will show us the way God is leading.

11

Three Ways to Make a Decision

Ignatian decision making is essentially the art of discernment applied to large questions. There's a methodology to decision making, and differences among types of decisions—all of which Ignatius discusses—but the heart of the matter is noticing and interpreting the thoughts and feelings caused by the movements of the spirits. This is true even for those decisions that get made primarily by thinking through the pros and cons by reasoning. Ignatius wants our minds and hearts to both be involved in decisions, but in the end he looks for the language of the heart to have a decisive role. The "heart" is the place where our emotions, thoughts, and feelings come together. The same art of discernment that shows you God's presence in your day is the discernment you use to make a major decision about your family or your next job.

Ignatius begins by telling us when we *shouldn't* make a decision. Some matters—marriage, priestly ordination—are unchangeable. One should "live well in the life he has chosen." Other matters are changeable, but that doesn't mean that we can assume that it's okay to change them.

> In matters that may be changed, if one has made a choice properly and with due order, without yielding to the

flesh or the world, there seems to be no reason why he should make it over. But let him perfect himself as much as possible in the one he has made.

If you've made a choice after making a serious effort to discern God's will, the presumption is that you should stick to it. This makes sense in terms of human psychology; our usual impulse is to think about making some kind of change when the going is tough. It also makes sense in terms of what we know about spiritual forces. One of the more alluring false consolations that the evil spirit offers is the idea that life would be much better if you did something different than what you're doing now. Ignatius says that we should view such notions with skepticism. We shouldn't reconsider a settled matter unless there is a good reason to do it.

Sometimes there *is* a good reason to do it. In fact, this happens often. Should I change jobs, perhaps even change careers? Should I go to graduate school? Should I pursue this relationship? Should I retire? If we're to consider making changes like these, God will take the initiative. God works through attraction; if it's time to make a decision, you will feel a persistent attraction to something else. If you don't feel an attraction—if you want something new because you're bored, frustrated, or disgusted with things as they are—put the question on the shelf.

The matter for a decision needs to be practical and real. A vague idea or longing for change won't work. The thought that "I really should do something to get out of this dead-end job" is not an issue for a decision. In this case your decision might be, "Can I make something more out of this job or should I find another one?" This might be the first of a series of decisions. "I'm leaving the job; should I stay in this field or switch careers?" "I'm switching careers; which of these possible fields is best for me?" And so forth.

WAYS TO MAKE A DECISION

Ignatius devotes a large section of the *Spiritual Exercises* to decision making, or "the election" as he called it. He has important decisions in mind, but the principles he sets down are good for decisions of lesser importance as well. He thought that a decision could be made in three ways. The first mode is the sudden, firm "no-doubt" decision—a revelation from God about the right path that leaves no room for doubt. Decisions in the second mode rely on classic discernment of the states of consolation and desolation. The third mode primarily involves our intellectual faculties, especially our reasoning and imagination.

Apart from the first mode (God's direct revelation), Ignatius describes two general approaches. One involves interpreting the feelings of consolation and desolation that we experience as we ponder our alternatives. It emphasizes the affective dimension. The other approach emphasizes the intellect. But these approaches are not exclusive. Our feelings and reason are both involved in decisions. We seldom make a decision solely on a "gut feeling," and our feelings are usually involved in decisions made primarily by weighing pros and cons with our minds. The difference between the two is mainly a matter of emphasis.

THE FIRST WAY: "NO DOUBT ABOUT IT"

The first mode is the answer that comes directly from God. You have an overwhelming conviction that one of the alternatives is the right one. There is simply no doubt about it. Ignatius calls it a "first-time" decision.

> **First Time.** When God our Lord so moves and attracts the will that a devout soul without hesitation, or the

possibility of hesitation, follows what has been manifest-
ed to it. St. Paul and St. Matthew acted thus in following
Christ our Lord.

This kind of decision is reminiscent of Ignatius's description
of consolation without previous cause in his rules for discernment. Sometimes divine grace descends on us without warning
"out of the blue." It isn't caused by something we see or hear or
think or remember. God touches us directly. Since only God has
direct access to our souls, Ignatius says that we can be sure that
this kind of consolation is from God. Sometimes decisions come
this way too; we just "know" what we should do.

The essence of this first-time decision is a compelling attraction that we cannot doubt. We're pulled to it "without the possibility of hesitation," says Ignatius. This seems to have been the
experience of St. Paul and St. Matthew, whom Ignatius points
to as examples. When Christ called him, Matthew, a tax collec-
tor, dropped everything and followed him immediately. When
Christ revealed himself to Paul on the road to Damascus, Paul
had no doubt about what he needed to do in response. He sur-
rendered his life to Christ. For both men, it was impossible to
doubt that Christ was showing them the right direction.

Does this happen very often? Probably not. We are sensory, reasoning, feeling creatures, and God usually works through
everyday circumstances and ordinary human faculties. On the
other hand, dramatic conversions are not unheard of, and it's not
unusual for people to have an unshakeable conviction that they
are being called a certain way. "I was born to teach." "I've always
known I should be a priest." "I've never wanted to be anything
but a doctor." Such certainties may well be a kind of Ignatian
first-time decision. Even so, people with these "no doubt about
it" convictions must make many more decisions as they pursue
their calls.

THE SECOND WAY: DISCERNMENT

If God doesn't give a "no-doubt" answer, we're to move on to the second way of making decisions. Ignatius describes it very briefly:

Second Time. When much light and understanding are derived through experience of desolations and consolations and discernment of diverse spirits.

Most of the time we are conflicted when faced with an important choice, and the conflict shows up in our feelings. One alternative seems attractive, but then we have doubts about it, and another alternative seems better. Misgivings creep in, and we decide that the first choice was better after all. But we're not sure. We are pulled back and forth.

Ignatius thought that this movement back and forth between consolation and desolation was the usual condition in the heart of a person trying to make a significant decision. When the matter is an important one, the struggle in our conflicted hearts will intensify. The good spirit and the evil spirit are active, and their work shows up in the unrest in our hearts. This is normal. In fact, Ignatius told spiritual directors to worry only when *nothing* seems to be going on in the heart of someone facing an important decision.

Usually *something* is going on. "Second time" discernment is about detecting the leading of the Holy Spirit in this ebb and flow of the inner life. Ignatius learned about it during the year he spent recovering from injuries. Recall what happened. He dreamed about returning to a life of romantic liaisons and swordplay; he also dreamed about becoming a great saint and servant of Christ. The dreams of derring-do left him feeling depressed and discouraged; the dreams of following Christ filled

him with excitement and joy. He recognized that God was leading him through these feelings. When we use discernment to
help make decisions, we are doing essentially what Ignatius did.

In one of his rules for discernment, Ignatius explains why
consolation and desolation are important for decision making:

> For just as in consolation the good spirit guides and
> counsels us, so in desolation the evil spirit guides and
> counsels. Following his counsels we can never find the
> way to a right decision.

In other words, consolation and desolation are not simply
spiritual and emotional states that we enjoy or endure. They
mean something because spiritual forces are active in them.
When we are facing an important decision, we can discern the
best path to take through careful discernment of these feelings.

We begin by *noticing* these spiritual movements. Usually, as
soon as we realize that we have to make a choice, we have some
initial reactions. We might be excited about a new possibility; we
might experience a wave of fear. The Examen prayer is a good
practice to sharpen our awareness of these feelings.

We need to decide what these spiritual movements mean
for our decision. Spiritual consolation and spiritual desolation
are not the same as feeling good or feeling bad. You might feel
excitement at the prospect of a new job because it will give you
the chance to travel to interesting places. Or you might feel sad
because you will miss your former colleagues. Surface feelings
such as these don't usually have much spiritual significance. (Of
course, if they are very intense, you might need to explore why
you feel this way.)

Spiritual consolation and spiritual desolation are deeper
feelings that affect our relationship with God in some way. They
involve the fundamental disposition of the heart. They contain

a sense of "rightness" and "wrongness." Spiritual consolation has to do with a sense that certain actions will take us closer to God and more fully realize what we truly desire. Spiritual desolation is a sense that we are getting away from who we truly are. When these feelings arise in decision making, Ignatius says that the good spirit and the evil spirit offer "counsel" through them.

The counsel of desolation isn't much help. God doesn't send desolation; feelings of distress, anxiety, and discouragement are the bailiwick of the enemy. In theory, we might learn some valuable things by discerning how the evil spirit is operating in desolation, but this is difficult discernment full of complexities. Ignatius's best advice about desolation is to resist it and ignore it for purposes of decision making. He warns us never to make a decision while in desolation, because in it we hear the counsel of the evil one.

We're most interested in the counsel of the Holy Spirit that comes through consolation. As you ponder the choices before you, be alert to feelings of joy, contentment, and peace. Look for that gentle (or not so gentle) attraction to one of the alternatives. It might be the Holy Spirit saying, "Go this way." It *might* be. Leadings from the Holy Spirit need to be interpreted and evaluated. There are complexities and nuances. There are many questions to ask about the counsel of consolation. Is the counsel a spiritual one—that is, is it rooted in faith and centered on God? Does the counsel really come from ourselves, as we read things into the afterglow of a pleasant experience? Is it a false consolation prompted by the evil spirit?

One experience of God's leading isn't enough. Ignatius says that "*much* light and understanding are derived through experience of *desolations* and *consolations* and discernment of diverse spirits." Plural. We can approach confidence that we know God's will as we have many experiences of the Holy Spirit's leading over time and in diverse ways.

Don't do this by yourself. Find a spiritually sensitive friend or counselor who can help you look at these matters objectively. You may have overlooked something important. The very process of describing your decision to another person is likely to help you understand it.

THE THIRD WAY: USING YOUR HEAD

There's a third way to make a decision if the first two don't suffice. This way makes particular use of our mental capacities, especially our abilities to reason and analyze. Here we're not looking for leadings from God during times of consolation, and we're not employing the classic tools of discernment.

There's a lively discussion among Ignatian specialists about how distinct the second and third ways of reaching a decision actually are. They're different; one relies on our affective nature while the other relies on reasoning. But in practice there's overlap. A second-way decision always includes some reasoning and a third-way decision involves the emotions at some level. The ideal in the Ignatian tradition is a unity of the will, emotions, and mind. All are present in a decision. The different modes are differences in emphasis.

Ignatius described the second way of making a decision in one brief sentence: "When much light and understanding are derived through experience of desolations and consolations and discernment of diverse spirits." He describes the third way in some detail. He sets forth preconditions, and offers two different ways to make a decision of this kind.

The first precondition is a time of tranquility—"*a time when the soul is not agitated by different spirits, and has free and peaceful use of its natural powers.*" In tranquility we are not experiencing consolation and desolation. The second requirement is to consider "for what purpose man is born, that is, for the praise of God our Lord and for the salvation of his soul." This is language from the First Principle and Foundation. There's another requirement: that we desire to do the thing "that would be more for His praise and glory."

The first method of making a third-way decision involves a careful weighing of the advantages and disadvantages of the alternative courses of action. Here's how Ignatius puts it:

> This will be to weigh the matter by reckoning the number of advantages and benefits that would accrue to me if I had the proposed office or benefice solely for the praise of God our Lord, and the salvation of my soul. On the other hand, I should weigh the disadvantages and dangers there might be in having it. I will do the same with the second alternative, that is, weigh the advantages and benefits as well as the disadvantages and danger of not having it.

This is a process of reasoning and analysis. We might envision filling in a chart with four columns: pros and cons of Option 1; pros and cons of Option 2. Once all the factors are down on paper, you ponder the matter deeply:

> After I have gone over and pondered in this way every aspect of the matter in question, I will consider which alternative appears more reasonable. Then I must come to a decision in the matter under deliberation because of weightier motives presented to my reason, and not because of any sensual inclination.

This is a very thorough deliberation. Ignatius wants us to consider "every aspect of the matter in question." We're to look at the question from every angle, consider every factor, go back and see if we've overlooked anything. We think about it, and then think about it some more. This implies a process that takes some time. In the end we're to make a decision based on what seems most reasonable. We examine the pros and cons, think deeply about them, and choose the alternative that makes the most rational sense.

The second way of making this kind of decision brings the imagination into the picture. Ignatius calls it a second way, but many experienced spiritual directors think that it's a supplement to rational deliberation. The big challenge in decision making, and in all discernment, is to be sufficiently detached from disordered affections so that we can see what we really want.

To help us achieve objectivity, Ignatius offers three imaginative scenarios. In the first we imagine that a stranger comes to us for advice. We don't know this person at all, but we wish them well and want to help them do the right thing. The stranger is wrestling with the same decision we're facing. He or she wants to "choose for the greater glory of God." We listen to the person explain the matter. What advice would you give? Which factors seem important? Which seem irrelevant? This exercise should help free us from the biases that cloud our judgment.

The second scenario has us imagine examining the decision from our deathbed. The third scenario is to imagine the same thing from the perspective of the Last Judgment. At the end of your life, the disordered attachments melt away. Your career, the size of your house, fancy vacations, your love life, concerns about money, honor, and power—none of this matters anymore. What do you wish you would have done about the decision you're facing? For example, money is very much on your mind as you consider several job offers, and rightly so. Your family needs an adequate income. But in the bird's-eye view of your life, *how* important is the difference in salary as compared to other factors in the decision? Again, the exercise is intended to help us achieve detachment—"without leaning to either side."

CONFIRMING THE DECISION

The final step is to seek confirmation of the tentative decision. Ignatius writes:

> After such a choice or decision, the one who has made it must turn with great diligence to prayer in the presence of God our Lord, and offer Him his choice that the Divine Majesty may deign to accept and confirm it if it is for His greater service and praise.

That's all Ignatius has to say about the matter. He leaves important questions unanswered. What counts as confirmation? How are we to seek it? How much time should we spend looking for it? It's even a bit unclear *why* Ignatius insists on confirmation. If the discernment process has been strong and thorough, why do we need *more* evidence to confirm a sound decision? The reason probably has to do with Ignatius's insistence on thoroughness. He believed that we should make every reasonable human effort to do our best. This means trying to find confirmation of an important decision so that we've done everything we can to find God's will.

Of course, what constitutes "reasonable effort" varies from person to person and circumstance to circumstance. Time runs out; a decision has to be made. Some decisions are more important than others. Prudence suggests that we shouldn't spend a lot of time seeking confirmation of relatively unimportant decisions, perhaps no time at all if time is short and other matters clamor for our attention. That's why there is no single answer to the question of how long we should take seeking confirmation. What happens if we've reached the limits of "reasonable effort" and no confirmation is forthcoming? In that case, says Juan Polanco, one of Ignatius's closest associates, we should go ahead and make the tentative decision final.

It's easy to skip this step—probably another reason why Ignatius insisted on it. Usually we want to move on after we've made a decision. If the discernment process has been a long one, we're glad it's over. We want to get on with the job of implementing it. No second thoughts, please. Ignatius says that we should pause at this point, present the decision to Christ, and ask for a sense of confirmation.

In most cases, confirmation comes in the form of consolation. Doubts and anxieties melt away. We feel at peace with the direction we've chosen. We have a sense of "rightness"—the decision we've made will take us closer to God, closer to what we really want.

One final thought about confirmation. Often people will say that the outcome of a decision confirms or disconfirms it. If things turn out well, that means that God wanted the thing to happen, and that the decision reflected God's will. A bad result means the opposite: God didn't want the thing to happen, and it was a bad or faulty decision. There's something to this idea. In the rules for discernment, one sign of a false consolation is the result of the actions taken under its sway. If people are angry about what you're doing, and if you're miserable and depressed, the consolation that led to your decision might well have been a false one. But maybe not. Ignatius points out that the forces of darkness oppose the work of God. If anything, obstacles, difficulties, and even outright failures are to be expected.

Another version of this idea is the attitude that "I'll go ahead with this plan, and God will stop it if he doesn't want it to happen." Sometimes—often—all we can do is push on and do what we think is best in the midst of uncertainties, time pressures, and partial knowledge of the situation. But the results don't say much about the soundness of discernment. The plan might fail because God didn't want it to happen. But it might also fail because Satan derailed it. It might fail because biases and self-seeking cloud the judgment of other people who have to make the plan work. It might fail for no obvious spiritual reason at all. The bank puts a freeze on mortgage loans. A better-qualified person gets the job you want. You might go ahead with your plan, but if it doesn't work out, don't say that God didn't want it to happen.

Future events will tell nothing about the soundness of a decision you are making now. You don't know what the future holds. You don't know what other people will do. You don't know what God wants other people to do. But with sound discernment, you can know what God wants *you* to do, now, in these circumstances. It will be a decision that will bring you closer to what you really want.

Final Thoughts

Ignatian discernment is full of surprises. It's a way of life rather than a set of rules. It gives us hints rather than facts, complexity rather than simplicity, questions along with the answers. It helps us along a journey. It doesn't take us to a place where we can pitch a tent and settle down.

It's remarkable how often writers who know a lot about discernment speak of uncertainty. Pope Francis is a good example. "If one has the answers to all the questions—that is the proof that God is not with him," he said. "If a person says that he met God with total certainty and is not touched by a margin of uncertainty, then this is not good." Uncertainty is a necessary part of discernment as Ignatius viewed it. Perhaps Ignatius's most disturbing insight is that the evil spirit might be behind our most "spiritual" thoughts and most altruistic plans. Things are not what they appear to be.

Uncertainty is built into the nature of things. Finding God in all things means that no doctrine, religious tradition, philosophical scheme, or devotional practice can exhaust the mystery that is God. We will never reach the end of "all things." Some things will always be hidden from us. But it's also true that something will always come along to make God present in a new way. There will always be surprises.

That's what we find in discernment—the surprises of the Holy Spirit, the infinite plenitude of God's blessings, descending on us like the rays of the sun. Discernment is becoming aware of these things. Ignatius insisted that the spiritual life should be something that is consciously experienced. We shouldn't allow it to descend into a routine that follows familiar paths. We're to look for God, notice his presence, respond to his call.

Ignatius insisted on action: "Love ought to manifest itself in deeds rather than in words." God has work for us to do. We practice discernment so that we can determine what this work is. It's serious business; much depends on it. Ignatius preached diligence; he insisted that we do as much as we can to discern well. But we're not to be anxious about this. It's all God's work. "Do not think that God our Lord requires what man cannot accomplish," Ignatius wrote to an anxious friend. "If one satisfies God, what difference does it make whether he satisfies men? There is no need to wear yourself out, but make a competent and sufficient effort, and leave the rest to Him."

Acknowledgments
and Sources

Quotes from the *Spiritual Exercises* are from the translation by Louis J. Puhl, S.J., published by Loyola Press. It is available online at *http://spex.ignatianspirituality.com/SpiritualExercises/Puhl*.

I found these books and authors especially helpful as I studied discernment:

Seek God Everywhere: Reflections on the Spiritual Exercises of St. Ignatius, by Anthony de Mello, S.J., Image Books, 2010.

Spiritual Consolation and *The Discernment of Spirits,* two books by Timothy Gallagher, O.M.V., published by Crossroad Publishing.

Weeds Among the Wheat, by Thomas Green, S.J., Ave Maria Press, 1984.

Understanding the Spiritual Exercises, by Michael Ivens, S.J., Liturgy Training Publications, 2000.

Discerning God's Will, by Jules J. Toner, S.J., Institute of Jesuit Sources, 1991.

Grateful thanks to friends and mentors who have very generously helped me: George Aschenbrenner, S.J.; Dennis Dillon, S.J.; David Fleming, S.J.; Bert Ghezzi; Ben Hawley, S.J.; Tim Hipskind, S.J.; Bernie Owens, S.J.; Daniel Schneider, M.M.; and J. Michael Sparough, S.J.

Chapter 2, page 24
"He is close to each one of you as a companion. . . ." Address of Pope Francis to the students of the Jesuit schools of Italy and Albania, Friday, June 7, 2013.

Page 25
"Let the risen Jesus enter your life. . . ." Homily of Pope Francis, Holy Saturday, March 30, 2013.

Chapter 4, Page 43
Prayer for me is always a prayer full of memory. . . ." "A Big Heart Open to God: The exclusive interview with Pope Francis," America magazine, September 30, 2013.

Chapter 7, Page 76
"I was held back by mere trifles. . ." Augustine, *Confessions*, VIII.11

Chapter 8, Page 85
"He cannot ravish. He can only woo. . ." C.S. Lewis, *The Screwtape Letters,* Chapter 8.

Chapter 10, Page 112
"Uncertainty is in every true discernment. . ." "A Big Heart Open to God: The exclusive interview with Pope Francis," *America* magazine, September 30, 2013.

Final Thoughts, Page 139

"If one has the answers to all the questions. . . ." "A Big Heart Open to God: The exclusive interview with Pope Francis," *America* magazine, September 30, 2013.